NORFOLK

Edited by Simon Harwin

GW00502189

First published in Great Britain in 1999 by
POETRY NOW YOUNG WRITERS
1-2 Wainman Road, Woodston,
Peterborough, PE2 7BU
Telephone (01733) 230748

HB ISBN 0 75430 299 7
SB ISBN 0 75430 300 4

FOREWORD

With over 63,000 entries for this year's Cosmic competition, it has proved to be our most demanding editing year to date.

We were, however, helped immensely by the fantastic standard of entries we received, and, on behalf of the Young Writers team, thank you.

The Cosmic series is a tremendous reflection on the writing abilities of 8-11 year old children, and the teachers who have encouraged them must take a great deal of credit.

We hope that you enjoy reading *Cosmic Norfolk* and that you are impressed with the variety of poems and style with which they are written, giving an insight into the minds of young children and what they think about the world today.

CONTENTS

Sean Jones	18
Oliver Dennis	18
Christina Goodwin	19
Martin Fairchild	20
Beccy Louise Matthews	20
Yanneke Whitehouse	21
Jeanie Baker	21
Bethanie Martell	22
Jeremy Wright	22
Charlene Folds	23
Philip Crowther	23
Sara Curtis	23
Becky Heavens	24
James Howard	24
David Lynskey	24
Clare Walker	25
Craig Ellis	25
Clare Moll	26
Martin Shreeve	26
Alex Johnson	27
Lee Haggith	27
Sami Bainham	28
Lisa Wright	28
Benjamin Willmott	29
Florence Watts	29
Holly Bygrave	29
Selina Garrard	30
Suzie Miller	30
Scott Townsend	31
Laurens Southgate	31
Hannah Burton	32
Alice Lupton	32
Ryckie Wade	33
Rachel Sage	33
Tom Leese	34
Scott Bumphrey	34

Louis Hudson	35
Abigail Horton	35
Lucy Whitwood	36
James Payne	36
Suzanne Fox	37
Roy Pooley	37
Benedict Goodwin	38
Sian Carter	38
Ben Hepworth	39
Becky Hitchens	39
Alexandra Edgell	40
Jack Davies	40
Laura Whitwood	41
Edward Woolston	41
Thomas Scrivens	41
Rebecca Usher	42
Amber Moll	43
Ben Watkins	44
Duncan Bradshaw	45
Michael Seaman	46
Esther Wright	46
Sam Bryant	47
Chris Pearce	47
Alice Brown	48
Rachel Mellor	48
Liam Hardesty	49
Lydia Burton	49

Corpusty CP School

Kayleigh Overton	50
Greg Brenchley	51
Hannah Carman	52
Nikki Thornton	53
Charlene Fisher	54
Catherine Perry-Warnes	55
Timothy Morgan-Evans	56

Jessica Davison   56
George Barber   57
Hester McDonald-Thomas   57
Hannah Brown   58
Amy Husar   58
Oliver Tyndall   59
Kyle Lovett   59
Michael Oldman   60

Docking GM Primary School
Ben Daniel Gage   60

Fakenham Junior School
Nancy Benson   61
Catherine Philpot   62
Kathryn Girling   63
Thomas Rose   64
Kirsty Andrews   64
Melissa Webb   65
Thomas Blaza   66
James Neal   66
Kerry Walden   67
Kyle Barnard   67
Sam Paul Walden   68
Charlotte Rayner   68

Grimston County Junior School
Hannah Valentine   69
Alex Jones   69
Grace Bennett   69
Charlotte Barrett   70
Lee Rasberry   70
Lucy Lovell   70
Thomas Lewis   71
Carley Tuttle   71
Catriona Oddie   71

Ben Howard	72
Abbie Rust	72
Victoria Buckingham	72
Carla Smith	73
Matthew Canfor	73
Rebecca Thorne	74
Justine Smith	74
Julia Chapman	75
Michelle Radcliffe	75
Dominic Widdows	76
Hayley Marie Burman	76
Katie Panks	77
Joshua Ayres	77
Jason Tuffs	78
Luke Harvey	78
James Curson	79
Rebecca Howard	79
Katie Kavanagh	80
Dominique Reeve	80
Pippa Armitage	81
Rebecca Jones	81
Emma Rallison	82
Mark Evans	82
Kerri Pightling	83
Sarah Townshend	83
David Hill	84
Oliver Stride	84

Hilgay Village School

Craig Everitt	85
Lindsay Peel	85
Natasha Williamson	86
Sarah Carter	87
Samantha Marie Walker	88
Katie Foreman	89
Victoria Fleming	90

Jonathan Reiss	90
Jamie King	91
Samuel Garcia	91
Liam Reynolds	92

Levendale Primary School

Megan Brette	92
Jenna Prest	93
Katy Opie	93
Amy Lawton	94
Vicky Bell	94
Rachel Simpson	95
Kathryn Jackson	95
Olivia Sudar	96
Andrew Grief	96
Paran Nithiananthan	97
Emel Bagdatlioglu	97
Lynsey Edwards	98
Carly Weeks	98
Stuart Stock	99
Lyndsay Pullan	99
Robert Edemenson	100
Jack Manning	100

Litcham CP School

Jack Harris	101

Mattishall Middle School

Jessica Warman	101
Elizabeth Wood	102
Daniel Harrold	102
Sarah Pearson	103
Kerri French	103
Sally Bangs	104
Ricky Gayfer	104
Gina Steggall	105

Middleton VC Primary School

Rory Harper	105
Lyndsy Thorpe	106
Jonathan George	106
Nicola Symonds	107
Thomas Seaman	107
Amy Gurney	108
Andrew Turner	108
Laura Footer	109
Maryann Watkins	109
Kaylee Petch	110
Sammy Reeks	110
Ben Partridge	111
Alice Rainbird	111

Northwold Primary School

Joanna Turner	112
Paul Preston	112
Dayna Cook	113
Ryan Spindley	113
Brownwyn Singleton	114
Tim Jolly	114
Jenna Waller	115
Amy Peckham	115
Francesca Eyles	116
Steven Milner	116
Abigail Chilvers	117
Samuel Ward	117
Michael Waring	118
Cara Taylor	118
Dale Ward	119

Norwich Road School

Rohan Jadhav	119
Shakira Simone Garrett	120
Joe Peaks	120

Ormesby Middle School

Andrew Dobosl	155
Maria Murphy	156
Lee Jeffries	157
Amanda Copestake	158
Thomas Hall	158
Ben Stone	159
Apryl Markham	160
Thomas Pearce	160
Avril Lacey	161
Kylie Hall	161

Roydon County Primary School

Ashleigh Rouse	162
Paul Mackmin	163
Melissa Eaton	163
Matthew Oxley	164
Sherree Larter	164
Lucy Harbour	165

St Nicholas School, North Walsham

Gus Eldridge	165
Rupert Smith	166
Oliver Brighton	167
Robert Bird	168
Leanne Ditch	168
Jennie Hall	169
Ryan Price	169
Caroline Chapman	170
Rachel Stone	170
Holly Dunham	171
Alastair Cockburn	171
Zoe Stennett-Cox	172
Benjamin Brown	172
Simmo Catchpole	173
Chantelle Prior	174

THE POEMS

A STORM AT SEA

The wind is blowing like a big fan,
The wind is whistling and howling,
The waves are towering up to the clouds,
Then crashing the boat as if it is going to break,
The sea is bouncing in horror.
The ship is thrown like a tennis ball,
It is tossing and turning as it waits to get out of the storm.
The boat is creaking as if the boards are going to snap.
The clouds are creeping across the sky, ready to strike with rain.
The people are running across the boat.
Men are shouting and trying to keep the boat stable.
Their oars are beating against the murky sea.
The rain is beating against the people's faces like lightning bolts
It is stinging them as if the Devil were scratching their skin.
The hail and wind weakens; the storm gets weaker and weaker.
The sea comes to a halt and the men cheer.
The clouds clear away and the sunlight shines on the boat once more.

Tristan Davies (10)
Aylsham Middle School

STORM AT SEA

The sea is smashing and bashing the boat.
The sea is being blown by a great giant.
The clouds are gathering up to get the boat.
People are shouting and skipping. A giant is pushing the waves.
The boat is getting battered.
The sky is a deep red as if it is haunted by devils and demons.
There's a god in the black sky waiting to strike the boat.
The storm is getting smaller and smaller and fades away and is
                                        then gone.

Louis Camilleri (9)
Aylsham Middle School

THE CRASHING SEA

The wind is blowing gently,
It starts to get rough and tough,
It starts to bash and crash against the boat.
Starting to get strong, the waves look like monsters coming out
of the sea.
The waves have got hold of the boat and are tossing and throwing
it across the sea.

People are shouting with horror,
They're frightened with despair.
The rain is tough and scraping across their faces,
The boat is creaking,
The waves are smashing against the boat,
The clouds are stalking behind them,
The sea is dark, grey and black, all deep colours,
The clouds are creeping across the sky,
The sea is surely tiring,
The men are anxiously putting up the sail,
The wind calms down. The men are relieved.

Camilla Davidge (9)
Aylsham Middle School

I BELONG

I belong on Earth where I was born
I belong with my family at home
I belong in bed
I belong in my secret laboratory (my shed)
I belong at school with my friends in 7B
I belong on Wednesdays at JYG
I belong with Aylsham Wanderers FC.

David Garlish (12)
Aylsham Middle School

A STORM AT SEA

The sea rose up like an angry ocean bear,
Crashing down on the ship sucking it under,
It then lets it go and tries again to suck it under the waves,
The storm rode on the grey horses,
Smashing down the rain like a thunderbolt,
Cutting the faces of the helpless men,
All the time the ship is losing the chess game,
Helplessly being bombarded as if it's going to break in the almighty
storm.
People praise the god, begging him to stop the blue, grey sea towering
over the ship and crashing down on it,
To stop the grey clouds throwing the rain down,
Slowly but surely their wish came true,
The blue, grey sea did stop towering over the ship and crashing down
on it,
Then the storm faded away slowly and the storm god went back to
his place in the sky.
The sea stopped tossing the boat around like a toy,
All was calm,
All was quiet,
The sun has captured the sky again.

Matthew Reeves (9)
Aylsham Middle School

HAPPINESS IS

Happiness is:
Football training on a Tuesday evening.
Playing on my bike after school.
Winning the house point trophy.
Beating everyone at badminton in the garden.
Going to the beach and swimming in the sea.

Matthew Hall (11)
Aylsham Middle School

A STORM AT SEA

The sea is rough and tough
The waves are smashing and crashing against the boat
The boat is groaning as if it is going to break
The clouds are creeping across the sky, turning grey to black
The sounds of the wind are roaring, whistling, howling, wailing
The rain is beating and stinging their faces
The boat is thrown by the waves
The wind is blowing them all over the sea
Then it begins to stop gradually
The sky is going back to blue
The wind is now calming down
The boat has now stopped groaning
The storm is over
We're safe again!

Caroline Owen (9)
Aylsham Middle School

THE STORM CAT

The storm is like a great sea cat waiting to pounce,
The sky is looming, waiting to drop and cover us in a black sheet,
As the storm cat gets angry, the waves draw up to meet the sky,
Then the storm cat pounces, bombarding the boat with blue, black
water,
The sun gives in and cowers behind a black coat,
The ship is thrown and tossed as if it is nothing but a model boat
on a huge ocean,
And then the storm roars again in desperation as it is about to die,
The wind is running away, away,
And then the storm cat sleeps and the clouds drift away.

Alex Glaister (10)
Aylsham Middle School

A Storm At Sea

The sea is rough, tossing the ship back and forth.
Left and right, battering and crushing the ship.

The wind is howling, crushing everything in its path except
The little ship in the middle of the sea.

People are shouting to each other; the rain is stinging against their faces.

The sky is towering over the ship, like a black cloak.

Bolts of lightning are shooting across the sky.

The storm is taking over.

It's as if the ship is trapped in a tiny bubble.

Gradually the storm begins to break;

Gradually it goes away.

Now it's peaceful; the sun shines brightly.

Wayne Overton (10)
Aylsham Middle School

A Storm At Sea

The wind is tearing and ripping the sail,
The waves are bombarding the ship, smashing and
                          crashing it as if it is a toy
The ship is thrown and tossed like a ball,
The rain beats on the people's faces,
The people are shouting orders,
The clouds creep across the sea as if they are wild cats,
The storm slowly dies down; the sea is calm again.

Luke King (9)
Aylsham Middle School

A STORM AT SEA

The clouds build up like a gang of robbers,
They grab hold of the ship and throw it afar,
The ship is tossed and thrown; it groans as if it's going to break,
The clouds creep across the sky waiting to destroy,
The wind is tearing down the deck, crushing everything in its path,
The waves tower high over the mast top then bombard the deck,
                                             crushing everything,
The clouds look like oil touching the low horizon,
People are shouting, giving orders to the crew,
The rain is thrashing on the poor sailors' faces,
The storm has died down but the wind keeps on howling,
Finally the wind is calm and the storm has gone,
The sea has returned back to blue.

Craig Barkley (10)
Aylsham Middle School

STORM AT SEA

The waves are throwing the ship about,
Tossing it as if it were in the storm's command,
The ship is getting pushed off course,
It is almost as if the storm is hungry,
The wind is whistling through the clouds which are creeping
                                             through the sky.
The storm is stalking and is ready to pounce,
The ship is groaning as if it were alive,
The people are shouting through the wind and the rain,
The storm and the wind are getting very rough and are defeating
                                             the crew,
The ship is giving up; it seems the storm has won.

Paul Wheeler (9)
Aylsham Middle School

A STORM AT SEA

The storm looms up above the horizon,
It's dark black, dingy green and dark sky green.
It roars and howls like a lion in pain.
The storm tosses the boat from side to side,
The men fall to the side and fight to hold on.
The violent spray of the ocean's waves smacks the boat angrily.
Men shout orders, 'The sail down. Turn left,' they cry worriedly.
The sky is grey, dark purple and black.
Thunder clouds are sailing across the sky sadly and dangerously.
Rain drums down splashing us, stinging our faces.
The boat is rocking wildly like a wild rocking horse
The people are scared but have given up crying for help.
The sky grows darker; the wind blows harder.
But we won't give up, we'll fight to the end.
Slowly the sea changes direction; the wind loses its strength,
The rain dies down to only a trickle, the sky turns lighter.
'We are saved,' we cry as we turn south and gently sail away.

Lucy Hardesty (10)
Aylsham Middle School

STORM AT SEA

The ship sailed soft and calm,
Merrily we went along,
There we rocked on the boat,
Suddenly a storm arrived.

It was scared, and terrified,
There were loud roaring winds,
There were loud roars of thunder,
There were big black blasts of rain.

Claire Townsend (10)
Aylsham Middle School

STORM AT SEA

The storm is groaning and smashing the sea.
The sea is crashing into the ship.
The storm is making lots of noise.
The sea is rough and bombarding the ship.
The sea is nearly meeting the clouds.
The rain is beating on the ship and stinging the men's faces.
The wind is whistling and howling as if it is being chased by a fox.
The people are shouting for help as though they're being kidnapped.
The sky is turning different colours like light blue to dark blue, then to
black.
The clouds are turning different colours like grey and black,
The ship is being tossed and thrown by the sea,
The storm is getting tired and weaker.
The storm is dying at last.

Stephanie Hall (9)
Aylsham Middle School

STORM AT SEA

The sea and waves meet the clouds,
The clouds creep across the sky,
The ship is thrown and tossed,
The rain beats on and stings people's faces,
It looks as if the ship is going to break,
The wind is whistling through the sail,
The clouds are as dark as night,
The clouds are grey and black,
The storm is dying,
The people are slowing down and the day
comes at last.

Ross Chamberlin (10)
Aylsham Middle School

A STORM AT SEA

The wind is rippling the sea as if it was a big snow storm.
The sea is bouncing up and down,
The colour is fierce green and dark blue,
The storm is looming above the horizon,
Clouds are pointing at the ship as fiercely as they can,
The violent storm is bouncing up and down,
It is making the men roll over,
The sea is going green and grey,
The clouds are looming over the ship,
The sea's making the boat break,
The men are calling to go in another direction,
The wind is losing its strength second by second,
At last the storm is dying and the sun is peeking out.

Emma Cornish (9)
Aylsham Middle School

THE GREAT STORM

The sea was like a humbling roar,
And the rain was like stones falling,
There were great flashes of lightning
                    striking the ship.

There were great balls of hail,
Whacking the sails of the ship,
There came a wave throwing itself on
                    to the ship.

The storm finished with just a calm and
                    normal sea
The flashes of lightning had gone
                    and the rain.

Andrew Fox (10)
Aylsham Middle School

A STORM AT SEA

A dark purple cloud is coming in like an eagle.
A roll of thunder is heard in the distance.
Lightning flashes, lighting the sky.
Winds are coming in, whistling, wailing, getting stronger
                                        by the minute.
Faces are stinging with rain.
The howling of the wind is heard clearly during the storm.
Waves are bashing and tearing along the boat.
People are yelling SOS. Their voices not being heard.
The sea is the colour of a cluster of seaweed.
The bottom of the boat is slimy and wet.
Then the clouds get lighter. It is dying away.
The boat stops being tossed!
The torn sails are up!

Rachel Northway (10)
Aylsham Middle School

A STORM AT SEA

The waves are towering over, then crushing on top of the boat,
The deafening wind is blowing in the faces of the crew,
The waves are so high that they reach the clouds,
Black clouds are creeping across the sky,
The sea is green, murky and black,
The sky is dark green, black and grey,
The wind is howling and whistling,
The people on the boat are shouting and screaming,
The rain and hail are beating and stinging on their faces,
The storm is dying and running away,
The storm is gradually dying and fading away.

Stewart Smith (9)
Aylsham Middle School

THE COLOURFUL BEETLE

Like a tiny rainbow,
It flies gracefully-silently,
Through the air,
Towards its prey,

Its shell is like a rainbow,
Glistening in the sun,
Reflecting like a prism,
Using the light from the sun.

The beetle rarely walks on the ground,
Because it likes to fly
It doesn't mind what time
Maybe day,
Maybe night.

Jack Robinson (11)
Aylsham Middle School

STORM AT SEA

The building storm is black and grey, hiding the sun with thick clouds,
The sea is indigo, jade, violet and grey,
The ship is creaking like loose floorboards; men are slipping on the
                                                                    deck,
The boat is being tossed and thrown about,
The rain is beating against the men's faces, stinging as it hits,
The wind is strong, blowing the people around on the boat,
The men are shouting on the ship,
They're scared they will be thrown overboard,
The storm is gradually dying; they are going to be safe,
After a while the storm goes away.

James Lee (9)
Aylsham Middle School

AUTUMN IS HERE

Autumn is here,
Summer is gone.

Crunching leaves,
Fall to the ground.

Bonfire night is
Coming soon.

Leaves turn colours,
Brown, red, orange.
Nuts start to drop off.

Bang look over there
Crackle, bang.

The night is still
One owl is hooting
It's pitch black.

Summer is gone
Gone far, far away.

Lucy Crook (10)
Aylsham Middle School

SNAILS

S nails are slimy and slow
N ow and then you see them
A gain on the wall
I   n a hole
L ost out in the dark
S nails are slimy and slow.

Callum Moorhead (10)
Aylsham Middle School

JUST THE SEA AND ME!

A crying love lost at sea,
Fierce, raging, angry with me.
Waves so great,
But yet full of hate,
Just the sea and me.
A big freshly shaken sheet,
Like a tiger ripping, attacking meat.
Bouncing up, crashing down,
Colours like diamonds on a crown.
Just the sea and me.
A dark shape bobbing on the horizon,
Like an old man trying to run,
Bumpy like a floor rug that's just freshly been spun.
Just the crying storm and me!

Beth Aquarone (10)
Aylsham Middle School

A STORM AT SEA

The great blue sky turned grey as if it was covered with a giant coat,
A storm loomed up above the horizon,
The calm sea turned rough and began towering above the ship,
The wind whistled as it soared through the sails,
The waves looked like green flames roaring and tossing over the sea,
As the waves crashed down; violent sprays hit all around,
The rain beat down, hitting and stinging as it fell from the sky,
Then the storm began to die as quickly as it came,
The coat was removed and the flames melted away,
The grey clouds sailed away and the boat rocked itself gently as if it
had been injured in a fight.

Siân Davies-Horne (9)
Aylsham Middle School

THE STORM AT SEA

We left the shore on a calm wave,
Seagulls sang as we dropped
Below our homes and ground level,
Sunset came with peace and quiet.

A breeze came and strong waters,
We started to be tossed around,
We were pulled along south
A crash of lightning came

Followed by flashes from the sky,
The clouds were blacker than black.
We were slipping across the deck,
The ship was being destroyed.

The water was over the ship,
The sails were torn and destroyed.
The whale's song could not be heard,
We pulled at the sails, it was hard.

The sea was starting to die down,
Rain no longer came down on the ship.
The blue sky was seen again and,
The song of the whales was heard.

Shayn Daniels (10)
Aylsham Middle School

MR BALONIE AND HIS PONY

Mr Balonie and his pony,
Sat and ate some cheese cannelloni
They sat in a chair and dried their hair
And thought they were very rare and fair.

Mr Balonie and his pony,
Had a friend with a bear called Tony.
They thought they would like this grizzly chap
But thought - No! When he ate their friend's cat!

Jezie Fredenburgh (11)
Aylsham Middle School

MY ROCKET

My huge rocket
gliding into the air.
Big balls of fire boom!
unto the air,
leaving a smoky grey
trail behind it.
Crackle, clatter went
the rocket as it was
leaving the earth.
Different colour gas
coming out of the rockets
behind.
Pinks, blues, reds, yellows
everywhere blowing
about in the wind.
The shiny door
sparkles and glistens
in the sun.
The people inside get
thrown about as the
bumpy rocket travels
into space.

Sarah Hitcham (9)
Aylsham Middle School

THE BIG STORM

We got on to the boat,
We went to set off,
The harbour cleared as we went,
With the calm sea below us.

We had gone for a while,
Something came to swallow us up,
A storm had come to get us,
I began to get frightened.

Flashes of lightning had come,
I tried to hide somewhere,
I was scared to my skin,
Suddenly everything stopped.

The waves stopped rolling,
The wind stopped whirring around,
We could hear the birds singing,
Everything was calm again.

Vicky Moss (9)
Aylsham Middle School

EVERY DAY IS A HAPPY DAY

Playing in the summer's sun
Scuffling into the soft hay,
Rolling and rolling in the squidgy mud
Watching the water running away.
Sleeping in the baby's pram
Pushing me up and down
Bouncing in the long grass;
Resting for the next day.

Louise Daniels (10)
Aylsham Middle School

STORM AT SEA

We came out the harbour,
On a lovely clear day,
The clouds were high in the sky
We did not fear, slowly they came over
They were coming closer.

The clouds were here,
The winds were coming over
Monstrous waves spraying over the ship
I was soaked through with water.

Our ship was getting tossed about,
This was the worst storm we had had
We were all falling over each other
Someone fell overboard.

The storm was getting calmer,
But it was still pretty bad,
The sky was as dark as the darkest night
The rain was coming down in torrents.

Alex Hudson (9)
Aylsham Middle School

THE CHASE

The fox started running as hounds chased them by,
Men on horses galloped across the forest,
As the brave fox tried to get away swiftly,
And then there was an almighty *bang!*
It got shot,
It stumbled then died,
Just outside its den.

Kelly Potter (11)
Aylsham Middle School

MY FRIEND IS . . .

My friend is like a ginger cat which lashes out at you.
My friend is as soft as sand which buries you - with ideas
My friend keeps me safe - like a car seat belt
My friend is as bright as a flood light with his brain bigger than his
head.

He's like a Dodge Viper - fast and slim
He roars like a Mercedes Benz - he's like a lion
He's like a rally car - skidding and turning.

My friend is like a computer that switches itself on and off.
My friend is as weird as a monkey that laughs at everything.
My friend is like a sniffer dog on the trail for drugs.
My friend is like a microwave that warms the inside of you.

He's like a little green army solder - a toy he so looks like.
My friend is Philip Crowther - a good and loyal friend,
He sticks up for me when there's trouble - and never tells a lie!

Sean Jones (11)
Aylsham Middle School

NUMBERS AND ALLITERATION

One weird, wonderful wasp.
Two terrible talking taxis
Three thirsty, thrilling thrushes.
Four frozen, famous forests
Five fine, female fire-fighters.
Six strong, straight stilts.
Seven stone, stubborn statues
Eight eager, evil eagles
Nine nasty, naughty neighbours
Ten tall, tearful tailors.

Oliver Dennis (10)
Aylsham Middle School

SCHOOL

As I walk to school I scuff my shoes along the floor,
As I get nearer to the door,
I rush to meet my friends,
As time gets nearer to the bell,
I chat with my friends, secrets we tell,
The bell goes,
And everybody knows,
To go and stand in line,
We go into school one class at a time,
When everyone's in,
The lessons begin,
First of all models we make,
Then we all go out to break,
I play with my friends,
Then break ends,
We go back into school,
Then we go to the swimming pool,
We go back for lunch,
My crisps I munch,
Next we have drama,
I pretend to be a llama,
Next we go to Mrs Kaths
I love it here because it's maths,
We line up outside the door,
I learn my tables up to four.

Christina Goodwin (10)
Aylsham Middle School

MY FRIEND IS . . .

My friend plays with me like a kitten.
He keeps me as safe as a lock on a door.
We two are like peas and carrots.
My friend has a sense of humour like a hyena.
He goes to the same school as me.
He's my best friend.
His name is Gary.

My friend looks out for me like an eagle.
My friend is as fast as a cheetah.
My friend can be trusted like the sun will shine.
He's as noisy as a revving car.
But I like him that way,
He's got to be Gary
My best friend!

Martin Fairchild (11)
Aylsham Middle School

MIDNIGHT

Lights are on it's nearly midnight,
Trees are blowing in the wind.
The dew has settled on the grass,
Now the clock strikes twelve.
The sky is drifting on the wind,
The rain is coming down
Hear the wind blowing, rain falling
Trees blowing side to side
Cats are fighting
Cars are starting
Now it's time for school.

Beccy Louise Matthews (10)
Aylsham Middle School

FRIENDS ARE FOREVER

Friends are forever
Friends help you
They care
And you will have fun
With your friends
You have memories of them
If you have a good time
That's what a good friend is
Neighbours are friends,
And people from school
Are friends as well
That's what a friend is.

Yanneke Whitehouse (9)
Aylsham Middle School

THE BADGER

Black and white
Stripes down to his nose.
Grey mottled with white.

Roams around the countryside
Hunting for acorns, berries,
Snails and beetles.

After a week the babies
Are born - and they come out
And play games together.
Sometimes the mother joins in!

Jeanie Baker (10)
Aylsham Middle School

MY FRIEND FERN

My friend is an animal,
But person quite alike,
She'll always go through anything,
No fence will put up a fight.
She has the radiance of a swan,
Graceful and still,
Her scent is like holly, jasmine and fern
Indeed that's what I called her!
Fern! like the morning dew,
Her fur is like silk and satin
Her nose and ears like pearls.
Me and her have two strong hearts,
We stick together like the honey to the bees
Fern and me!
And we stretch forever like the river to the sea,
Fern and me!
Even if she is small, and I am big,
We are quite alike,
Even if she is a guinea pig!

Bethanie Martell (10)
Aylsham Middle School

I BELONG

I belong to Earth everyone's' world.
Aylsham our town where I live.
My name the one that Mum and Dad gave me.
My cat because I look after and love her.
My cricket team and football team.
My family my mum, dad, sister, grandmas and grandads
Our God who looks after us and loves us.

Jeremy Wright (12)
Aylsham Middle School

ME AND MY BEST FRIEND

My friend sticks up for me - like a pack of Meercats.
My friend has a sense of humour - just like a hyena
My friend and I are about the same size
Like two giraffes walking side by side.
My friend and I live near to each other
Like two monkeys in different trees.
My friend and I are always together
My best friend's name is Beeky . . .

Charlene Folds (10)
Aylsham Middle School

MY FRIEND IS . . .

My friend has a sense of humour like a monkey.
My friend is as loyal to me as a dog is to his master.
My friend always keeps us safe like a merecat on the look out.
My friend warns me if there is trouble or danger, like a gerbil.
He is as fast as a Mini but as cool as a Saab 9000.
He is as close to me as the paintwork on a Ferrari
My friend is Daniel.

Philip Crowther (11)
Aylsham Middle School

HAPPINESS IS . . .

Writing a poem in the evening,
Listening to music on the radio,
Seeing my friends at school,
Reading my book in my bedroom,
Seeing my gran at the weekend.

Sara Curtis (11)
Aylsham Middle School

MY FRIEND IS . . .

My friend is as loyal as a dog is to it's master.
My friend looks after me like a horse does its foal.
My friend has a sense of humour like a hyena.
My friend makes me feel as safe as a locked door.
My friend cheers me up like a comedian cheers up his audience.
My friend would walk through fire for me.
My friend is my Mum . . .

Becky Heavens (11)
Aylsham Middle School

MY FRIEND IS . . .

My friend is loyal to me like a dog on a lead.
If there's trouble he sticks up for me like a lion in a cage.
My friend is as close to me like a puma to his cubs.
My friend likes the same things as I do
Like an eagle to it's prey.
My friend has a sense of humour
Like an orang-utan - swinging from tree to tree!

James Howard (11)
Aylsham Middle School

MY FRIEND IS . . .

My friend is as tough as old leather.
My friend is as calm as still water.
My friend is as fast as a cheetah.
My friend is as cool as an ice cube.
My friend is more to me than anything!
My friend's name is Jamie . . .

David Lynskey (10)
Aylsham Middle School

THE MAGICAL BIRD

There once was a magical bird
Who really was very absurd.
I heard that the magical bird
Likes cake with lots of lemon curd.
This pretty young magical bird
Is friends with a black cat who purred.
This pretty young magical bird
Does play the piano - I heard.
A fine horse has spread the word
That notes the bird plays are slurred
But that is all that I have heard
Of the fine young magical bird.

Clare Walker (10)
Aylsham Middle School

THE GHOSTLY HOST

There once was a ghost
Who made a good host
He liked to eat toast
Mostly on the coast
The ghost was a host
So he needed a post
The ghost made the most
Of being a host
But then on the coast
He was made to roast
And that was the end
Of the ghost as a host!

Craig Ellis (11)
Aylsham Middle School

SCARBOROUGH FAIR

There once was a girl called Clare
Who went to Scarborough Fair.
She rode on her beautiful mare
Which had beautiful golden hair
She ate an iced cake at the fair
And gave a carrot to her mare!

They met a young horse call Bim
Who loved to do cartwheels in the gym
One day he got a bad limb
And had to give up his gym
Soon he became very slim
And went to a race to win!

Clare Moll (11)
Aylsham Middle School

MY FRIEND IS LIKE A CAR

My friend is as cool as a Ford Cabriolet
With no roof on it!
He's as fast as a Formula one Ferrari.
He's as loyal to me as a car is starting first time in the snow.
We are alike as two Scanias built on the same day.
He lives as close to me as a steering wheel is to the dashboard.
He sticks up for me like a seat belt keeps you safe
And I do the same for him!
When we argue it's like two cars crashing.
But we always make up like a garage that fixes a car.
And we're still friends now . . .

Martin Shreeve (10)
Aylsham Middle School

A VINTAGE CAR

There once was a glistening vintage car
That got covered in sparkly thick *tar!*.

There once was a glistening vintage car
That drove into a wonderful old *bar!*.

There once was a glistening vintage car
That made lots of posh people shout *hoorah!*

There once was a glistening vintage car
That made the driver drink some English *char!*

There once was a glistening vintage car
And when children saw it they said *tar! tar!*

There once was a glistening vintage car
That got covered in sparkly thick *tar!*

Alex Johnson (10)
Aylsham Middle School

THE GHOST

I knew of a ghost
Which had a fat host
They lent on a big post
And ate a slice of toast
He went to the coast
He saw an orange post
There was a ship ahoy
Who had a fat toy
That was the ghost of Tom!

Lee Haggith (11)
Aylsham Middle School

CAT

Softly padding on velvet paws,
Towards the fire.
Her eyes are enchanted pools of light,
Blue as the sea.
Her whiskers are silver thread,
Gleaming in the moonlight.
Queen of the carpet,
Her sleek fur feels like silk.
Stretching her claws out,
They have the ability to hurt,
But she is a gentle creature.
Her tail twitching,
She peacefully purrs like a ticking clock.
She lazily lies down,
Comfy as a cloud.

Sami Bainham (11)
Aylsham Middle School

STARS

The stars are far away
They come out after day
The stars are far away
The stars shine best in May
The stars are far away
High in the sky they lay
The stars are far away
With a big shining ray
The stars are far away
Colour of a sandy bay.

Lisa Wright (11)
Aylsham Middle School

OH! LOOK AT THE WORM

Oh! Look at the worm
And how it does squirm
Oh! Look at the worm
And how it does turn
Oh! Look at the worm
Going for a meal of fern
Oh! look at the worm
Still has a lot to learn!

Benjamin Willmott (11)
Aylsham Middle School

THE SPARKLING DIAMOND BRIGHT

The sparkling diamond bright
Twinkles in the night
The sparkling diamond bright
So beautiful and white
The sparkling diamond bright
Twinkling in the moonlight!

Florence Watts (10)
Aylsham Middle School

TRISH

There once was a lady called Trish
Who liked to eat fine tuna fish
Trish ate off a very flat dish
On the dish there was tuna fish
Trish was granted just one wish
She wished for more tuna fish!

Holly Bygrave (11)
Aylsham Middle School

THE SNOWCAT

As quiet as a mouse,
The Snowcat comes.
As quick as lightning,
As white as snow,
Claws like needles . . .
The prey comes closer.

Prey prowling unaware of the Snowcat's
Icy stare!

Eyes like emeralds,
A tail like a snake,
Whiskers like violin strings,
Teeth as sharp as razors,
Nose like a black button,
Paws, padding patiently . . . He pounces!

Selina Garrard (11)
Aylsham Middle School

THE MOON

Quietly rising the moon
Awaiting her quiet doom.
Quietly rising the moon
Will silently die so soon
Her night
Takes flight
When the sun finally appears
It's the end of the moon's still years
Quietly dying - the moon
She has faced her quiet doom!

Suzie Miller (11)
Aylsham Middle School

Swan

As the beautiful creature moves down the
singing stream.
A hook just misses the graceful swan as it
moves in a dream.
He takes off from the lake with his plane
like wings.
It lands with its ash-like feet and its body as
white as untrodden snow.
Its eyes are bright as the sun in the sky.
His hook-like neck bent down for the fish,
he misses and tries again.
He delicately dipped a snake-like neck
into the depths.
He makes his way home and feeds his young.

Scott Townsend (11)
Aylsham Middle School

A Hunting Hawk

There was a hunting hawk
Who swallowed lots of chalk
And that stalking hawk didn't walk
And that hawk didn't talk
And he ate with a fork
And he lived in York
And he couldn't eat pork
He just looked at a cork!

Laurens Southgate (10)
Aylsham Middle School

HAMSTER

A hamster is as soft as silk,
It climbs about its cage like an acrobat,
A hamster's eyes glitter like sapphires,
Its claws are like needles,
A hamster silently sleeps in its soft bed,
And it moves like a tornado.

A hamster plays like a happy child,
A hamster is a happy harmless little hider,
A hamster is as quiet as a mouse,
A bubbly little hamster busily burrows tunnels,
A hamster is as cuddly as a soft toy,
A hamster is somebody's pet.

Hannah Burton (11)
Aylsham Middle School

THE SWAN

White as untrodden snow - she floats along like a cloud
on the still water.
Her eyes black as coal sparkle like the stars
as she silently sails on the smooth lake.
Her feathers smooth as silk and white as marble
she swam smoothly down the singing stream.
Wondrous wing beats whipping up the whooshing
waves that sparkle like sapphires in the sunlight.
She rose to the air - flying flawlessly in the fragrant air.

Alice Lupton (12)
Aylsham Middle School

THE RHINOSAURUS

The Rhinosaurus is a
Home in itself.
Like a moving mountain
It lumbers around
Looking for a shady spot to sleep.

Its horns are natural weapons
Which are poached for fun.
Its skin like flexible metal
Which keeps out most harm.

The grasslands are their homes,
They have been for hundreds of years.
If we could just live in harmony
The world could be a better place!

Ryckie Wade (11)
Aylsham Middle School

MY POEM ABOUT MY BLACK CAT

My black cat is as black as coal
His eyes sparkle like the stars in the sky.
He snores, he roars like the rumble of the earth
And hunts like the great hunter of the night!

My black cat is as fierce as the night draws on
He is still my knight in shining armour to me
But I love him so!

Rachel Sage (11)
Aylsham Middle School

SWAN

The swan glides gracefully across the lake.
He is the master of catching fish.
With his downpipe neck,
His wings like blades,
Cut through the air.
As he sweeps across the land.
His feathers as white as snow,
As they shine in the sun.
His beak as orange as carrots,
His legs as powerful as his wings.
As they push water aside.
He is the swan.
He is the king of the lake!

Tom Leese (12)
Aylsham Middle School

CHEETAH

Spots as black as charcoal,
Like coal on yellow topaz.
Eyes like binoculars,
Whiskers as sharp as needles,
The predator is out to catch its prey.
Speeding superbly across the oasis,
Finally attacking its prey,
Now trying to keep it away from other cheetahs.

Scott Bumphrey (12)
Aylsham Middle School

THE CAT: THE MOUSE

The cat, by the fire
Its glossy coat glistening,
Like stars on the sea.
Creak! Creak!
Soft paws upon the floor
An ear twitches, listening, listening
The cat turns its head
As slowly as pork on a spit.
A mouse scampers across the floor.
Its ears flapping like sails in a wind.
Watching wickedly with wild eyes.
The cat crouches
Watching! Waiting!
Suddenly the cat pounces as high
As a building block - upon the mouse.
The cat, by the fire,
Creak! Creak!
Its head spins round as quickly
As a propeller
But it is only the owner dishing out supper!

Louis Hudson (12)
Aylsham Middle School

LION

A lion has fur as golden as the sun.
He has pride for being
King of all kings.
He is known as the sleeper of all sleepers.
The roar he roars is like the Almighty
God of animals has awoken.
Stride after stride he runs from the gun!

Abigail Horton (12)
Aylsham Middle School

THE ROBIN

The robin sat quietly on
the old oak tree.
Red breast glistening in the sun.
Eating a bread crumb.
Feathers as soft as a pillow.
He flew off into the sunset,
Wings beating softly.
Flying through the darkening sky.
It was dark, the moon
Was shining down on him.
Eyes glistening - he went back
to the old oak tree.

Lucy Whitwood (11)
Aylsham Middle School

THE ANT

Here is the ant,
Body as black as night.
Delicately dining on a dandelion.
It spots a predator trying to catch him
And moves machine-like through mounds,
Smoothly swinging through stones.
Then the ant runs into the safety of his own home.
He has won! The predator lost!
Here is the ant
Busy as a bee
The quickest creature there could be!

James Payne (12)
Aylsham Middle School

A SEAL PUP POEM

Skin like silk,
Eyes that twinkle like stars.
Blubber like jelly,
Voice like an angel.
Flippers like hands,
Nose like a button.
Moves like a fish,
Graceful and beautiful.
Swimming smoothly in the deep blue sea.
A playful creature.
Fur as white as snow . . .

Suzanne Fox (11)
Aylsham Middle School

THE SWAN

The swan swims as gracefully as us.
The swan's wings are as wide as planes.
The swan's feathers look like snowdrifts.
The swan's feet are as grey as ash.
The swan's eyes are like gems.
The swan lands like a plane.
The swan drifts slowly across the lake.
The swan flies smoothly.

Roy Pooley (11)
Aylsham Middle School

THE SWAN

The swan is a king, ruler of the lake.
Powerful, majestic; Gliding through the water.
The white of its feathers stand out
Against stormy grey skies.

The swan is a killer,
Brutal and strong, a warrior afraid of nothing.

The swan's wings are a galleon's sails.
The swan is a storm cloud,
Soaring through the large sky.

Benedict Goodwin (12)
Aylsham Middle School

A CAT

Her feet are as dainty as a just fallen feather,
As she walks towards the fire.
Her eyes sparkling like sapphires
And her tail a strong rope swinging to and fro.
Her fur shining, all silky and smooth
Glistening in the moonlight,
And her nose, a pearl - soft and white.
I hear her peaceful purring,
As she drops soundly off to sleep.

Sian Carter (11)
Aylsham Middle School

A RIVER OF MIST

I move around the river of mist,
It moves and changes all the time.
It curls and wriggles around my yellow boots
And around my head.
Lights!
Two bright lights appear; A car passes
And then is consumed by the monster's grey mist.
I start to see faces in the grey surrounding,
So I run!
I run and run till I see the safe bright lights.
It is my home.

Ben Hepworth (11)
Aylsham Middle School

A SWAN

The dark water carries the graceful swan along.
The moonlight shines into its eyes.
His feathers gently rustling in the wind.
His face, a smooth cloud.
Delicately drifting down the stream.
A peaceful call echoes into the calm night.
Then weaving through the whispering
Reeds, disappearing out of sight.

Becky Hitchens (11)
Aylsham Middle School

A GOLDFISH

Its beautiful gold body
Swims in the water
Towards the ocean.

Its skin is scaly
Its eyes are pitch black
Like midnight.

Its tail is like a rudder
Steering it
In the right direction.

Alexandra Edgell (10)
Aylsham Middle School

TIGER

The tiger's eyes were like coal
Burning in the fire.
His jaws were set like mousetraps.
His claws glinting in the sun-like silver knives.
His prey could not see him for his zebra crossing body.
Then suddenly, like a bullet from a gun
He pounced and killed!

Jack Davies (11)
Aylsham Middle School

HAPPINESS

Happiness is . . .

Going to swimming after a busy day at school,
Playing tennis on warm Tuesday evenings,
Going to the rec for a football match,
Netball on Monday afternoons,
Visiting my friend Laura on Wednesdays.

Laura Whitwood (10)
Aylsham Middle School

THE DOG

It runs around the garden
It goes indoors and lies in its basket
It sometimes just sleeps
Or lies around the home.

The dog moves around slowly
About the garden.

Edward Woolston (11)
Aylsham Middle School

HAPPINESS IS . . .

Football training on a Saturday morning.
Playing cricket on the green.
Watching TV when I'm bored,
Eating sausages, chips and beans.
Getting no homework.
Weekends!

Thomas Scrivens (10)
Aylsham Middle School

ALPHABET POEM

A dders that slither along the ground.
B adgers come out at night.
C amels that have one or two humps.
D eer with white spots.
E lephants that *never* forget.
F oxes with long bushy tails.
G oats with horns and they are grumpy.
H amsters in the wild - running very fast.
I nsects creeping all around.
J ellyfish white and sting you.
K angaroos with their young.
L adybirds red and spotty.
M aggots that eat apples.
N ewts swimming around.
O ctopus with that ink I wanted!
P onies eating grass and galloping around.
Q uails that look like partridges.
R abbits hopping around.
S nakes slithering around.
T adpoles being born.
U mbrella birds looking like an umbrella.
V ampire bats - why do they hang around?
W hales big and bolshie.
X ylophagous - a group of animals.
Y aks with thick fur.
Z ebra - stripy black and white.

Rebecca Usher (9)
Aylsham Middle School

ALPHABET POEM

A lligators wallowing in the swamp,
B eavers swimming in the steam.
C ows munching grass hungrily,
D olphins jumping in and out of the water.
E lephants swaying along in the jungle.
F oxes dashing around in a coat of red.
G orillas big black and hairy - sitting in a tree.
H ippopotamus big, fat and grey having a drink.
I bises carefully perched on a tree.
J ackals laughing and running away.
K oalas hanging from eucalytus trees.
L adybirds spotted with black.
M onkeys swinging through the trees.
N ightingales singing in the darkness.
O striches glide gently - running at top speed.
P eacocks show off their brightly coloured feathers proudly.
Q uails fly overhead.
R abbits soft and fluffy thump their feet.
S nails slide through the garden.
T urtles swimming underwater.
U mbrella birds show off their crests.
V ultures swoop onto their prey.
W hales let up a puff of water.
X enopus frogs hop around.
Y aks trundle around in their thick coat.
Z ebras run around in their coat of black and white.

Amber Moll (9)
Aylsham Middle School

MY MUMMY SAYS . . .

My mummy says that that bike is -
A diamond-back bike
An expensive bike
A shiny bike.

My mummy says that that bike is -
A viper bike
Does it bite?
Can it slither through grass!

My mummy says that that bike is -
An arrow head bike
A sharp bike
A lethal bike.

My mummy says that that bike is -
A butler's bike
Does it serve drinks?
Does it spill them!

My mummy says that that bike is -
A mongoose bike
Does it quack?
Does it have feathers!

My mummy says that that bike is -
A universal bike
A planet bike
An alien bike.

No! It's my bike
And you're not having it!

Ben Watkins (12)
Aylsham Middle School

WHY I'M LATE . . .

Please Mr Earp, don't be cross;
I'm late because
I missed the bus.
This time it wasn't my fault - truly!

Last night dad brought a puppy home,
We called him Sam, he's a little beauty.
But he's starting to roam around
And get into all kinds of mischief!

He pulled the threads
From the rug on the wall.
Scratched the patterns
From the kitchen wall.
Savaged the curtains
Chewed dad's slippers
Ate the kippers
We were going to have for tea.
Then fell asleep in the coal bucket!

'That dog needs exercise' said my dad.
But he didn't have a collar or a lead.
So I went to buy them this morning.
'And buy some feed' said dad.

That's why I walked
To school today;
My legs are aching
It's a very long way.
That's how I came to
Miss the bus!

Please Mr Earp
Don't be cross!

Duncan Bradshaw (11)
Aylsham Middle School

MEMORIES

If I was stranded on a desert island
I would take these memories with me.
When I first went to Banham Zoo when I was three.
When I first drove a motorbike,
I got my first budgie,
The first time I went on an aeroplane.
We got a family dog when I was five.
I first saw my sister
I was at nursery school.
The first time I rode my bike without stabilisers.

Michael Seaman (10)
Aylsham Middle School

HAPPINESS IS . . .

Reading a good book in a sunlit garden,
Football training on Saturday mornings,
Playing tennis on school afternoons,
Enjoying netball on Monday evenings,
Having a stress-free day.
Riding my bike up and down the road,
Visiting my friend Sara on Saturdays.

Esther Wright (10)
Aylsham Middle School

I BELONG

I belong to my family.
My pets and
My house.
I belong to my friends.
My school
And the world.
My football team
In Aylsham
On my bike!

Sam Bryant (11)
Aylsham Middle School

BELONGINGS

I belong to planet earth because I was born here.
To my family I belong because I live with them,
I belong to my house because I know it well.
To my street I belong because I know everyone.
I belong in 7B because I was put there!
To my friends I belong because I see them a lot.
I belong to my brother because he's in my family.
To my pets I belong because I look after them.

Chris Pearce (12)
Aylsham Middle School

THE LION

Its big and powerful like a cat.
It has big black claws as sharp as knives.

Its mane is big and golden
It can be as fast as a jaguar
Its eyes are brown.

It creeps up to its prey
It chases a zebra
It pounces on its back!

Alice Brown (10)
Aylsham Middle School

MEMORIES

Going on holiday to France
Hearing that my Auntie has had a baby.
Going on holiday to Ireland.
Playing with my 3 year old cousin.
Going on holiday to Scotland.
Being a bridesmaid at my Auntie and Uncle's wedding
Going on holiday to the Isle of Wight
Moving into my new house.

Rachel Mellor (11)
Aylsham Middle School

BELONGING

I belong to
My house because it's nice and warm,
My bed because it's nice when I'm tired.
Our country because it's where I was born,
7B because that is my class,
My pets because they need me,
Aylsham because it is the town I live in,
Scouts because I am invested there and
I belong to earth!

Liam Hardesty (12)
Aylsham Middle School

MEMORIES

My friends - Laura, Laura, Hannah, Amy, Larissa, Holly and Gemma.
Becoming best friends with Laura Whitwood.
When I was picked to swim for my school.
Getting my tortoise-shell cat.
When I was picked to play for the Norfolk Girl's Football Team.
My Family.
Going to Ireland to see my cousins,
Laura coming round my house and dressing my sister's doll up in her
clothes.

Lydia Burton (10)
Aylsham Middle School

GARDEN

I gaze out of my sunlight-reflecting window
At my barren garden.
At spindly little twigs which once were
Beautiful blossoming bushes.
This was winter's doing.
Winter had come like a ravenous wolf
Tearing up everything in its path.
I wonder what it's like underground?
Warm, cosy?
The seeds urging to burst into blossoms.
A thousand colours,
But the seed needs water, light, and food.
The seed pushes its puny shoot against the heavy soil
Searching desperately for light.
It is determined to have a life above ground.
Slowly, a green shoot appears.
Days pass, the plant grows healthily,
Taller and taller. Stronger and stronger.
Its bright green leaves spreading and unbending
Their little bodies.
Many happy days, blossoming in the sunlight,
Blowing in the breeze,
Watching the birds feed their young.
But after months winter returns
Spreading its ice-cold fingers and shattering icicles into the
Warm-hearted soul.
The plant begins to die, drooping its sorrowing head.
After a while it's all gone
But underground, new seeds are waiting
Ready to renew the life cycle once again.

Kayleigh Overton (11)
Corpusty CP School

Into The Wilderness

A swift breeze blows a hard little seed
Out of its crispy mother.
It is carried by the strong air.
The wind dies down
And the little seed lands
On rich damp soil.
A child's big footstep
(Or big to the plants of green)
The big caterpillar-gripped shoe
Pushed the seed under the damp soil.
A week went by.
The little seed broke its case like a baby bird
Breaking through its shell.
It pushes its succulent shoot to the
Heavenly light and air,
Twisting its powerful spine
Getting stronger and stronger
Every day.

Six months pass.
Winter is here.
Jack Frost spreads his ice-like fingers
Between every thread of grass
And places crumbly bread-like snow
On every leaf.
He drops his head in sadness
And once more the breeze blows
Into the wilderness.

Greg Brenchley (10)
Corpusty CP School

MAN

His eyes hidden behind his dense glasses
And his mouth lost for words
As his bushy ragged eyebrows
Blow in the howling wind
Like a pigeon being tossed around
In a winter gale.
His tie flutters about in the wind,
In despair.
You can see he's hiding something
But he doesn't show it,
To anybody.
Down the dark narrow street
His nose sniffs
In the cold and misty morning air.
He gives a hard stare
At the people who walk past.
Not saying a word
He chucks an empty can
In anger and frustration
He has no friends to talk to,
To look up to,
He sighs in despair.

Hannah Carman (10)
Corpusty CP School

HOMELESS

As I walk through the
Snowy, soundless streets,
I stop
And look around me.
I can see
A huddle of miserable, homeless people.
How must they feel?
How can I ever know
With the silvery flakes floating
Down from above.
They shatter on the floor
As if they were made of crystal.
They all stare at me,
With their faint pale faces.
I try to imagine
What the sanitised streets look like
Beneath the thick, white blanket of snow.
When starving children shiver
They look at me with their
Cheerless, gloomy eyes.
Not knowing what is next in life.

Nikki Thornton (11)
Corpusty CP School

SWEEPING ACROSS THE SKY

An owl perched on top of an oak tree.
It looked as though the old branch
Was about to snap in half.
I walked a step and stood on a twig.
The twig snapped.
The startled owl swept across the sky.

A mouse was hiding in the corn when
The twig snapped
The startled animal ran
Clattering through the yellow corn.
Above the field the owl turned its head.

Sweeping down
The dagger-like talons stabbed
Into the back of the small creature.
It snapped like a twig.
It was all over.
Picking it up, blood dripping on the ground,
The owl swept up into the oak tree.

Charlene Fisher (11)
Corpusty CP School

COMING TO TAKE ME AWAY

The wind sounds like a calling wolf
        Coming to take me away.
I hear it coming through every crack
        Coming to take me away.
It prowls in the night giving me a fright
        Coming to take me away.
He creeps through the wood following my scent
        Coming to take me away.
He scrambles through hedgerows and weaves
through trees
        Coming to take me away.
His fingers are frozen his breath is frosty
        Coming to take me away.
He blows soft crisp snow like sparkling
fireworks falling to the frozen ground
        Coming to take me away.
I know he's out there somewhere,
Out there somewhere.
        Coming to take me away.

Catherine Perry-Warnes (10)
Corpusty CP School

WINTER

It's cold, very cold.
The snowdrifts bury
The lives of many.
The evidence of passers-by
Lies dead in the snow.
Chimneys spewing poisonous smoke.
Choking the air like an assassin,
Bringing death to children.
They play gleefully with snowballs
Unaware of winter's downside.
Nature is at rest while predators search.
Homeless shadows lie in the back alleys.
In city streets they sleep the sleep of death
While more fortunate families
Celebrate Christmas
Ignorant of the fact that
There is no Christmas for the poor.

Timothy Morgan-Evans (10)
Corpusty CP School

WINDLESS

It was windless so that it could grow into the sky with the real sun,
So there could be two suns just like there should be.
Then it came up with a burst and a cracking and
I jumped back as the new sun came up out of the darkness
Into life.

Jessica Davison (10)
Corpusty CP School

AUTUMN SUN

Morning grass,
Tipped with white frost.
An early morning mist
Forming as the sun rises.
The late morning breeze
Whisks the ochre leaves off the trees
Making the earth golden brown
In readiness for the cold night.
Birds flock under the yellow sun.
The wind, its time over, dies away
Allowing bonfires to be lit
Adding warmth to the afternoon sun.
Teatime, and the sun departs
After its brief visit.
Allowing the moon to rise
In a cold clear sky.
Silence shattered by an owl hooting.

George Barber (11)
Corpusty CP School

ALL ALONE

The gloom of whiteness in the great silence of snow.
With a black, dirty face a little terrified girl
Scrambles through the dustbins all covered in downy snow,
As if in search of a lost heart.
In the bitter, cold wind, soft snowflakes float by her sad eyes.
Homeless and with nowhere to go
She sighs and lies down in the soft cold snow.

Hester McDonald-Thomas (10)
Corpusty CP School

CRISPY LEAVES

You walk on the leaves.
They crack like breaking bones.
You pick up a leaf.
How crisp it feels.
Like tin foil.
You see the sun.
The big fiery orange in the sky.
You walk amongst the trees.
You hear animals scurrying
About like they are in a rush.
You hear the wind blowing.
It sounds like chips
Sizzling in a pan.

Hannah Brown (11)
Corpusty CP School

SCARLET GIRL

The wide smile on her face shows that she is happy,
Or is it just the act she has to play?
The lightning flash of the flash bulb,
Then her face calmly relaxes.
Her hair is as yellow as a misty sunrise.
It is tucked carelessly behind her ears.
Her skin is a haunted, pale, creamed whiteness.
Her eyes are as blue as the Mediterranean Sea
And her teeth are as white as the marble on a temple.
Her jumper, as scarlet as a crushed raspberry.
Her icy silver necklace is a chain that
Imprisons her in the camera's view.

Amy Husar (9)
Corpusty CP School

STARVED

The owl flutters into a small valley
Using the light of the moon
To search for voles and mice.
All he can find is carrion.
The remains of a rabbit
That the fox had left after it had retired
In search of better prey.
The owl hovers
Over a freshly-ploughed field
In hope of finding a tasty rodent.
The starving owl pushes the cold air behind
As it swoops back to the nest
To feed its chicks.

Oliver Tyndall (11)
Corpusty CP School

WINTER

Winter is deadly cold.
It strikes children like daggers.
Dig your car from its snowy grave.
Snow falls like running white
Horses on a track.
Snowmen live and then they die.
Icicles hang like eagles' talons,
grabbing mice and shredding
Them to pieces.

Kyle Lovett (11)
Corpusty CP School

FEAST

The rolling crimson sun floated and sank
In the enchanted sapphire sky.
The barn owl glided swiftly across the clouds
Looking for prey. Suddenly he spots a field vole.
The predator swooped down low immediately.
Too late.
The vole fled from the attacker.
Giving up on the vole the white-breasted
Owl landed on a branch.
Almost simultaneously a sparrow landed too,
Unaware that he was about to be eaten
By the silently approaching owl.
It walked up behind the unsuspecting sparrow and
Clutched it in its talons.
They curled around the sparrow and ripped the flesh.
The owl began to feast.

Michael Oldman (11)
Corpusty CP School

SUN

Nothing can stop the blazing beams reflecting from the
freshwater streams.
Everything awakened from its rays.
Getting the world ready for one of those days.

Ben Daniel Gage (11)
Docking GM Primary School

PARADISE

Although you are nearly as low as the
Water in the gutter beside you,
You feel as high as the sun yet you have the urge
To carry on, as fast as you can.
You imagine you are swinging through a thriving rainforest,
You hear bumble bees gathering nectar
From crimson-coloured flowers,
But in your rainforest they are exotic dragonflies,
Humming in the leaves around you.
You sense young children playing beside you,
And then decide they are a group of monkeys,
Some gently grooming each other,
While others cheekily swallow bananas whole,
You watch them slide down inside them,
Looking like an extra-large Adam's apple in their throats.
The monkeys don't give you a second glance,
As you continue to roar through the lush trees and vegetation.
Then you are suddenly awakened by a
Rough 'n' tumble kind of hand shaking you,
You have been stolen from your paradise,
Now you are in the park again.
It's someone else's go on the swing.
As you leave the park gates
You wonder what they imagine
When they leave the safety of the ground!

Nancy Benson (11)
Fakenham Junior School

THE GREEN MAN

In winter he sinks, groaning into the ground,
He makes a frightful noise which fades as he sinks.
He stays until he feels and smells the March frosts.
He jumps and springs upon his muscly, lush green legs.

He smells like the vegetation of a rainforest
As he walks he unsettles the frost
With his damp and musty scent.
Bulbs push their fingers above the earth.

He looks like a green monkey,
Stubbly brown twigs for fingers and toes.
Vines twist about his arms and legs
Like old, gnarled branches.

He is as old as the earth
With hair like brambles and lop-sided beard.
He's never shaved it off
It trails behind him.

He's strict with polluters of the world,
He finds his way to punish them
With poisoned mushroom and strangling ivy.
He's the unknown hero of the planet.

Catherine Philpot (10)
Fakenham Junior School

ALONE

All alone in the world
No one to care
Every time you wake quiet is all you hear,
No one to speak to or to hear
Alone in a crowd
Walking away from the crowd
Into a field as the lush green grass slowly moves
As the red burning sun hits the ground,
All around cows and sheep roam and graze,
The green grass moves with no sound.
Slowly I move on,
Now close to the cows
I see the black bull
Charging towards the gate.
Suddenly it stops and walks back to the herd of cows.
I open the gate,
The grass feels like feathers,
I lie down,
The sun feels hot as it hits the ground.

In the distance I see trees, a lot of them close together
now I do not feel alone because I am with nature.

Kathryn Girling (10)
Fakenham Junior School

SHARK

I live in the ocean, in a dark dark cave,
I am mighty strong and very very brave.

I eat other fish and some mammals too,
My teeth are so sharp that I don't have to chew.

I weave through the corals at the bottom of the ocean,
I track down my prey with a silent motion.

The shape of my body helps me swim with great speed,
I swirl in and out of the long seaweed.

I swim for miles in the ocean so cold,
I suppose I'll keep swimming even when I grow old.

I fight for my life, in anger and hate,
When caught on a hook loaded with bate.

There are many sharks with different names,
But if you caught one you couldn't call it tame.

At the sight of my fin people fear for their lives,
But I'm not all that bad, I'm just trying to survive.

Thomas Rose (10)
Fakenham Junior School

HANDS

Hands are caring,
They comfort you at night,
Mum's hands hug you,
Hands are soft and gentle.

Hands of an artist paint,
They paint fields with footsteps,
They paint the bright summer sun,
Hands paint beautiful pictures.

Hands are brilliant for Olympics,
Discus-throwing, he throws it and it hits the winning spot,
The winning of Wimbledon tennis tournament,
Hands are good at sport.

Hands are evil sometimes,
Lashing out hitting people,
Hands are evil holding guns,
Hands are evil because they can kill.

Kirsty Andrews (11)
Fakenham Junior School

THE PYLONS

These great towering monsters stand tall
Across the countryside hungry for power,
Strolling soldiers standing up right and important,
Destruction of the landscape is their game.

Giant bare skeletons, their bones humming.
Dangerous, life-threatening, stretching for miles,
Extending as far as the eye can see,
Vast chunks of metal dotted around.

Pushing their way through field after field,
Gigantic frameworks spoil everywhere for everyone,
People try to disguise them as trees,
But that doesn't work.

Some people like them because they light us,
Keep us warm, but why can't we route them underground?
Hideous things that will be around forever.
These are the future.

Melissa Webb (10)
Fakenham Junior School

ORLANDO THE CAT

I can see a familiar door red with windows
no letterbox.
I walk into the porch
My rollerblades on the floor with the shoes.
I walk into the hall I can see my brothers watching TV
through the door.
Coats hanging on the banister like monkeys
hanging off trees.

Outside there is a miaowing and a scratching.
I open the door and in comes Orlando
brown with white bits,
the paws white.
Orlando does a figure of eight between my legs.
I stroke Orlando, he has short hair like an eyebrow.
I get Orlando a saucer of milk,
He makes a slurping noise when he drinks as he laps.
I open the door and Orlando runs out.

Thomas Blaza (9)
Fakenham Junior School

EASTER

Easter is a time
To tell each little
Chick
To break its shell
To come into the
Warm sun
To see its
Mum.

James Neal (9)
Fakenham Junior School

I HATE IT

White lights everywhere.
Crackling as a firework.
Banging like a drum.
Shocking in a bang.
It's like feet stamping on the floor.
It could even break a window.
It's even louder than a bomb.
It's only just started but it is really frightening.
Shouts in the distance
As louder and louder it bangs.
I feel like it's World War III.
At last it's over.
What a relief!
Probably it's fed-up with complaints
So that's why it's stopped.

Kerry Walden (8)
Fakenham Junior School

A SPRING FEELING

Fields smell fresh
Clouds turn into animals
The grass is soft and it tickles my feet
The trees are big so birds make a home
There are birds that sing
Water splashing with the wind
Bees hum like cars
Squirrels spring from branch to branch
Butterflies float down like leaves
Then all is silent
Except a hum from a bee.

Kyle Barnard (10)
Fakenham Junior School

PYLONS

Pylons, like an army of skeletons
With bones that do not rattle.
Imprisoned by wires so they can't move.
They kill like soldiers, an army of death.

They catch unawares the people of the air;
Kite flyers, birds, gliders.
A sudden flash, as if from heaven
Ends their lives.

As you watch the sunset
This beastly framework blocks your view,
Making the countryside seem hideous.
People hear their humming
Ruining Mother Nature's sounds.

Sam Paul Walden (10)
Fakenham Junior School

MY SWEET LAND

The wind blowing in my face.
Bright blue clouds and an indigo sky.
The chocolate river tastes so sweet as I'm sailing along in my
Chocolate boat with its sail made of bubble gum
Orange leaves fall to the ground with the whistling wind
I jump off the boat and land on the peach-coloured grass
Trees as tall as flats covered with apples and pears.
Strawberries in patches, berries on bushes.
Fountains made of candy spurting lemonade
Cottages made of all things nice, sugar, candy, marzipan fruits
And out of the chimney comes fluffy candyfloss
Flowers made of lollipops
Fields full of all I've ever dreamed of in my sweet sweet land.

Charlotte Rayner (11)
Fakenham Junior School

WHALES AND DOLPHINS

Blue whales are big and long,
Killer whales are strong,
Dolphins play all day,
But they don't come up in the bay.

Hannah Valentine
Grimston County Junior School

WHEN I WENT TO SANDRINGHAM

One day I went to Sandringham
But I didn't see the Queen.
We went round the house and museum
And saw maps of places that I have never seen.

Alex Jones (8)
Grimston County Junior School

PETEY

Turtles, terrapins and tortoises,
I really do love them,
And little tiny Petey,
He is my best friend.

Grace Bennett (9)
Grimston County Junior School

UNTITLED

There was a spider called Sue
Who needed to go to the loo
She couldn't get in
So she went to the bin
And ended up doing a poo!

Charlotte Barrett (8)
Grimston County Junior School

UNTITLED

There was a flea called Lee
Who was a jumper like me
He went to the fair
But lost all his hair
So then he came home for his tea.

Lee Rasberry (9)
Grimston County Junior School

DREAMLAND

A pearly white unicorn,
Grazing gently in a dream.
Along comes a hunter,
It's not what it seems.

Lucy Lovell (11)
Grimston County Junior School

RAIN

Black clouds
Sure sign of rain
Slowly it gets harder.
Soon it's jumping five foot.
Gushing down gutters.
Splashing on tiles.

Thomas Lewis (10)
Grimston County Junior School

BOO!

On a dark and stormy night
Three witches stared with all their might
Two little ghosts said 'How do you do?'
The wizard went tip-toe, tip-toe.

> *Boo!*

Carley Tuttle (10)
Grimston County Junior School

UNTITLED

There was a little bee called Laura
Who ate a whole tub of Flora
She felt a bit ill
Took a giant pill
And ended up a bit poorer.

Catriona Oddie (9)
Grimston County Junior School

SNOW

It's blowing then it starts snowing
Let's go outside
And hide under the slide.
It's snowing, the wind is blowing
Let's make a snowman.
I went inside through the hall
Then I went out to make a snowball.

Ben Howard (8)
Grimston County Junior School

BOATING

Some people want to go boating
because they know that the boat
will stay floating,
but my experience on a boat
made me shiver like a goat.
It does sound silly I agree
but you wouldn't want to be me.

Abbie Rust (8)
Grimston County Junior School

SKY AT NIGHT

The soft owl hooting
A lonesome cat
Man walking down the street
Something sharp, red.
Sirens speeding past
What's going on?

Victoria Buckingham (10)
Grimston County Junior School

Sea Breeze

Sitting down talking
In the breeze,
Having a cup of tea.
The boats coming onto the land,
The smell of the fish.
I am walking down to the sea,
Sitting down on the sand.
Goats looking,
Goats eating the olives on the trees.
Sunshine burns your skin,
The sea nice and cool.
There's a bit of wind,
The sand blows in my eyes,
When I lie on the beach.
You can see the hill on the other side,
People with hats on
To keep them cool.
The green leaves
Falling to the ground.

Carla Smith (11)
Grimston County Junior School

The Lonely House

The lonely house standing by itself
The creepy house not even the sound of a mouse
It gives me the shivers throughout my body
I feel cold when I walk past
The broken pavement outside the gate
The creaking floor as the wind blows
The lonely house standing by itself.

Matthew Canfor (10)
Grimston County Junior School

WATCHING HER

Sitting looking at her go round
In her wheel.
Round and round as mad
As she can.

Seeing her eat her food,
So quiet as she holds it
In her paws.

My hamster is funny when
She's in my hands.
She loves me.
Her eyes are dark and they
Stand out.

She hangs on with one paw,
Loving and beautiful,
Quiet when she drinks.
Lovely.

Rebecca Thorne (11)
Grimston County Junior School

MY DEN

It was light, made of sticks,
It was open but began to close in on me.
The smelling of drains,
It was near a field,
Crossed streams
And went into an arch.
Few people knew.

Justine Smith (11)
Grimston County Junior School

MY DREAM

Splash! The waves, the children laugh and scream.

The children play in the sea, see some fish
Then they scream.

The sun up there at its best.
Susie's mum loves her vest.

The smell is nice
Kerri's eating some rice

Blue, green, black and yellow.
The sea is nice and shallow.

The sand is soft
The birds are lost.

The waves go crash.
The children splash.

Julia Chapman (11)
Grimston County Junior School

THE STORM

It is a stormy day
The wind is rough
The rain pours down
It is a stormy day
I heard a wolf howling
Then the TV flickers
It is a stormy day
The wind is rough.

Michelle Radcliffe (11)
Grimston County Junior School

SCRUFF

I imagine the moonlit field,
My dog going mad waiting to be let off,
My dad lets him go and he is gone,
Like a bullet from a gun.

My dad calls him back,
He steams across the field,
Back to sit down beside my dad,
I run across the field,
My dad lets him go,
He chases towards me,
I put him on the lead.

We leave the moonlit field,
All dark and dead,
Like a graveyard full of smoke.

Dominic Widdows (11)
Grimston County Junior School

CHILDMINDER!

A childminder screaming loudly,
Red raging with a headache,
In a house,
In the dark,
In a chair,
Alone with the baby
Pulling her hair getting ready
                          to go mad.

Hayley Marie Burman (10)
Grimston County Junior School

AUTUMN LEAVES

Autumn leaves
rustling all day
Children
kicking them as they go out
to play.
In the winter
no fun at all.
When it comes to spring they go back
to school.
It comes to autumn
again
and other people complain
except the happy kids who liked the
autumn.

Katie Panks (8)
Grimston County Junior School

MY CAT

My cat is really stupid
She thinks she is a monkey
She also thinks she is a hunter
My cat is really stupid
She doesn't like cat food
But she loves spaghetti
My cat is really stupid
She thinks she is a monkey.

Joshua Ayres (10)
Grimston County Junior School

INSPECTORS

Teachers try to be calm
Inspectors mooching around
Interfere with children
Glare at displays.

Teachers try to be calm
Inspectors scribble in their folders
Turn their nose up at our work
Inspectors get in the way.

Teachers try to be calm
Inspectors ask questions
They just sit around
Inspectors! We don't need them!

Jason Tuffs (10)
Grimston County Junior School

SCHOOL IS BORING

School is boring,
All you do is work,
Maths, English, science.
School is boring,
I don't want to go,
The best time is the end,
School is boring,
All you do is work!

Luke Harvey (10)
Grimston County Junior School

THE LIFE BEHIND A MASK

If I could wear a mask
It would have to be quite good.
It would have a good personality
And be nice to everyone.
The life behind a mask
I think it would be quite good
Especially being someone else
That I would like to be.
I wouldn't like to be behind a
Mask for the rest of my life.
But I think just a day will be
Quite nice.

James Curson (9)
Grimston County Junior School

DOLLY IS ALWAYS FUSSING

Dolly can't stop fussing
The teacher is really mad
She's good at her maths
Dolly can't stop fussing
She's always getting lines
But when she does maths she can't stop chatting
Dolly can't stop fussing
The teacher is really mad.

Rebecca Howard (10)
Grimston County Junior School

SNOW

The snow flaking from the sky,
Dropping down on us as we play,
Cupped hands scooping it up
The snow flaking from the sky
People forming snowballs, chucking
Them at each other playfully.
Looking out of the window seeing
Roofs white.
The snow flaking from the sky
Dropping down on us as we play.

Katie Kavanagh (11)
Grimston County Junior School

A BOO HOO STORM

One night a storm came along,
And rattled boats and people's coats.
In the morning the men's hopes had gone.
One night a storm came along,
And ruled the sea.
Poor men at sea.
One night a storm came along,
And rattled boats and people's coats.

Dominique Reeve (11)
Grimston County Junior School

A Tied Knight

A tied knight,
With a pale face,
Glistening silver armour,
In the dead of night.

A twig snaps,
As he steps,
He sees something in the mist,
But he ignores it,
Eventually he walks on.

Pippa Armitage (10)
Grimston County Junior School

The Rain

Falling, hitting the ground, like mice running by.
Splashing down into puddles.
The rain gets faster,
Falling hitting the ground like mice running by,
The rain stops,
It starts again more powerful than before,
Falling, hitting the ground like mice running by,
Splashing down into puddles.

Rebecca Jones (11)
Grimston County Junior School

THE NASTY SIAMESE

A spiteful Siamese cat
hissing by the cat flap
dribbling as he goes.
Dangerous prey for a warning
waiting to catch a rat.
An old box up in the rafters
there in the shed.
Dare to go in there
you'll be in for a scare!

Emma Rallison (10)
Grimston County Junior School

THE CREEPY HOUSE

The creepy house that's down my road,
I think it's haunted but I don't know,
I don't see why they don't knock it down,
The creepy house that's down my road,
My friend went in he wet himself,
It's so spooky he was nearly scared to death,
The creepy house that's down my road,
I think it's haunted but I don't know.

Mark Evans (10)
Grimston County Junior School

THE TICKING CLOCK

The clock ticking,
The dog sleeping,
I feel the wind in my face,
I shut the door,
The dog gets up limping,
What's wrong?
I feel my heart beating,
Silence, apart from
The clock ticking.

Kerri Pightling (11)
Grimston County Junior School

THE MASK

If I could wear a mask,
It would be a good task.
My behaviour could be fun
I would be very kind behind a mask.

Every day I would say,
'My mask will blow away.'
When I have so much fun,
I am wearing my old friend mask.

Sarah Townshend (8)
Grimston County Junior School

A DOG

I sit there, still.
But something else is with me.
I look out the window.
Nothing.
Something is moving nearer,
Entering my loneliness.
A dog sniffing around.
Small excited,
But limping tiredly.

David Hill (11)
Grimston County Junior School

INSPECTION

Inspectors go around
Asking questions they do
Interviewing the teachers
Writing in their notes.

Inspectors go around
Looking down and around
You get nervous
But more for the teachers.

Oliver Stride
Grimston County Junior School

THE DEATH OF BOUDICCA

One freezing day Boudicca
Demanded to her warriors
'We will go to war with the rotten Romans.'

All her warriors said 'March on!'
I'll fetch our weapons and armour
They all marched off together
Boudicca was leading.

They marched into the woods
Chanting as they walked
Deer stared at them as they marched by.
Children cheered them on.

Colchester grew nearer
They felt nervous and tense
There was a bloody battle
Loads of warriors were killed.

   The Romans won,
    Boudicca died.

Craig Everitt (9)
Hilgay Village School

ROCKING CHAIR

He is a rough brown rocking chair
He is a monkey
He is 3 o'clock because it's the end of school
He is red and dark blue
He is Coca Cola
He is rain and falling leaves.
This is Paul King.

Lindsay Peel (10)
Hilgay Village School

A LATE-NIGHT VISITOR

I hear a scrape
I wake with a fright
I feel my shocked heart
Thumping madly in the night.

Clench my fist
The light disappears
How can I sleep?
I can't hide my fears.

I can't ignore it
And go to sleep
But something is pulling me
To take a peep.

I see wet black fur
Cursing yellow eyes
Just beyond my window
The deadly creature lies.

I take a breath
I hear the gale
I screw up my eyes
My heart could fail.

I grip the curtains
Holding on tightly
Should I pull them?
Yes, just lightly.

I see razor-sharp teeth
Blood on its face
Glowing eyes
It wants a race.

I ran.
The creature grew a pink glow
I grew impatient
I heard a rocket, going slow.

I stumbled back to bed
It was one o'clock
Before I fell asleep
I pulled down the window

Locks!

Natasha Williamson (9)
Hilgay Village School

THE WINDOW

From my window I can see trees, road and river.
Against the trees leans fresh air waiting to be swallowed.
Beyond all this I can see fields green and houses dull.

After these there are all the places I long to be in.
Between hills and meadows bright flowers grow.
Behind these new words are brewing and crying as they
wait to be heard.

Beneath all of these small insects scramble and play around.
Above these planets rule the universe.
Behind these factories pour out pollution.

In through my window I can see a bed, books and ornaments.
Between book covers, pages overflowing with words.
Over the bed a light hangs, shining brightly.

Among ornaments dust sits on shelves.
Above the soft toys a pretty fan hangs.
Over in the corner a mess-free zone.

By a wall, a desk stands.
Against the shelves a pinboard leans.
After the curtains have been drawn the window acts like a mirror.

Sarah Carter (11)
Hilgay Village School

MIDNIGHT PHANTOM!

Tiptoeing
Towards the sounds
Teeth chattering
Hot flushes coming and going
Clock ticking as the pendulum swings
I try to hold back but something
Drives me on.

Eyes growing
Wider and wider
PJs growing tighter and tighter
As I sweat and get closer
To the sound from the window
There's a black figure moving
With wind.

Fists clenched
Teeth as sharp as spears
Head all round and pointed
Bright purple *eyeeees . . . ?*

Samantha Marie Walker (10)
Hilgay Village School

THE DEADLY BEAST

I reach for the key
To open the window
It's staring at me
Two eyes staring
Big and round
Slimy tongue
Licked its lips
I quickly ran and
shouted 'Mum'
The horrible beast
went away.

Sleep, dream,
          school, home.
I'm back in my warm bed.
          I'm nervous.
Will it come again?
I saw the beast again in my dream.
When I got in bed I had to scream.

Katie Foreman (11)
Hilgay Village School

THE STRANGEST TIME

One wet day Boudicca shouted to her warriors
'Come on, let's go to fight the rotten Romans.'
All of her soldiers said 'Come get your helmets
And your hard clothes on.'
They all climbed the hill together.
Boudicca was leading them.
Near the woods they shouted a war cry.
Colchester grew nearer.
There was a bloody battle.
Tons of people wounded and injured.
The Romans won.
Boudicca ran in the wood and ate some poisonous
Berries and died.
They would never forget their queen.

Victoria Fleming (9)
Hilgay Village School

THE DARK NIGHT

You're in your bed
Something's scratching *outside!*
Something in your head says
'Open the window'
You open the catch,
Only blackness and cold.
Quick.
Shut it. Go back to bed.
Dozing off.
The scratching starts again.

Jonathan Reiss (8)
Hilgay Village School

THE TEDDY SHADOW

Tap at the window
Hiding under my covers
I shiver, it goes down my spine.

Curtains not drawn
Black shadow appearing
Knees weak.

Eyes half-closed
Towards the window
I open the curtains
My teddy sits there.

Smiling at me!

Jamie King (10)
Hilgay Village School

FRIGHT NIGHT!

Going to bed tapping at the window
Louder, softer, louder, softer, I'm scared
Door slams shut.
Scratching windows, my body soaked with sweat.
Wind blowing, trees swishing.
Rattling floorboards.
Knees weakening.
Eyes wide and staring.
I'm fainting.
Crash!

My body on the floor!

Samuel Garcia (10)
Hilgay Village School

FROM DUSK TILL DAWN

Scratching at the window-pane
Creeping to open the window
Am I insane?
The eyes getting bigger.

Time to go
It would say
Time to go
Its hairy arms reaching.

'Go away!'
But it would stay
'Go away!'

'Why? just be friends'
'Why didn't you say so?'

Liam Reynolds (9)
Hilgay Village School

DEEP DARK CAVE

As I walk towards the deep dark cave I feel
like a block of ice in the Antarctic.
Echoing voices carry on as I walk through
the dark and misty cave,
As dark as a staircase without any light.
The walls dripping as if it was raining inside
Squishy and squelchy mud beneath my feet
making me slip and slide.
As I listen I hear squeaky high-pitched voices
fading into the distance.
I keep walking feeling as if this tunnel
is endless.

Megan Brette (11)
Levendale Primary School

DEEP DARK CAVE

As I walk into the tunnel it is lonely and
dark all around us.
As slippy as frozen ice, as wet as a
swimming pool, and as scary as monsters.
As darkness draws near, and as hopeless I feel.
And as calmly and sticky as toffee.
As rocky as a solid stone, the dripping walls
make me feel empty inside.
The darkness draws near as I walk further
away from the mouth of the cave, and as
dark as death, waiting round the corner.
As I walk through the cave I suddenly
realise that it is getting mistier and mister
all the time. At last the mist in the air
fills me with joy everywhere.

Jenna Prest (10)
Levendale Primary School

A DEEP DARK CAVE

As I go in I slip on the icy rock.
The cave is a desolate and empty desert.
When I speak my voice echoes from
                    cold, dark, dripping walls.
It then draws me into its pathway of darkness.
Then I finally come out into the bright light.

Katy Opie (10)
Levendale Primary School

A WINTER WORLD

We make snowmen in the
winter.
It is so much fun.
You should come with us.
There is so much to be done.
We look at the winter day.
I wish it could be May.
The snowflakes fall.
The icicles hang on the wall.
The ice is solid.
The snow is hard.
Now it is dark we all go inside.
We look out of the window,
Until it is bedtime.

Amy Lawton (8)
Levendale Primary School

DEEP DARK CAVE

The gloomy dark cave was pulling towards me,
I was abandoned in the moist and creepy cave,
The frightened dusk made me tremble with fear,
The alarming, grimy and silent cave walls were
                                    coming in on me,
The dew-brushed walls were slimy and dull,
The darkness wraps around me and takes me away.

Vicky Bell (11)
Levendale Primary School

A WINTER WORLD

Clear icicles hanging from
ledges.
White snow is falling down to
the ground.
The wind is blowing in a whirl.
Views of snow are wonderful.
Children are building snowmen
in the deep snow.
Trees sparkle with the snow,
Snowmen with carrot noses and
stone eyes stand as still as
soldiers.
Ice on the puddles make
beautiful patterns.

Rachel Simpson (9)
Levendale Primary School

DEEP DARK CAVE

As I enter the cave I think I will never come out
The gloomy inside of the wet damp cave
I think I'll never see light again
The eerie echo of me as I talk is magnified
A thousand times.
The clammy sticky wall catches me tight.
The stalagmites and stalactites catch me in their maze
I feel relieved as I come out into the sunlight.

Kathryn Jackson (9)
Levendale Primary School

WINTER WORLD

People are shivering and
shaking.
Animals are hibernating.
The lake has frozen.
The holly has bits of snow on.
Icicles hang from rooftops.
People build snowmen.
Children go on their sledges
down a hill.
Leaves fall from the trees and
crumble.
People ice-skate on the frozen
water.
Robins eat berries.

Olivia Sudar (8)
Levendale Primary School

WINTER

In winter, the frost and snow
cover town and country.
Icicles grow from the drips
on the window ledges
And hang down from the
lamp posts.
They curtain the entrance to
the badger's sett.

Andrew Grief (8)
Levendale Primary School

DEEP DARK CAVE

As I walk in the morning sun I see a cave
towering over me, with fog bellowing out of its
huge mouth.
I feel cold in the damp, dark, desolate cave
The air is freezing in the bare empty chambers
of the foggy cave.

When I talk it echoes off the slimy walls.
The sound of bats chittering in the glum cave
The enchanted, shiny, stalactites hang from the ceiling.

At the end of the cave, a lonely hole greets me,
I step out into the bright sunlight,
the cave looking enchanted.

Paran Nithiananthan
Levendale Primary School

A DEEP DARK CAVE

I feel as if I am trapped in the frightening dark hole.
I feel lonely and hopeless in the dark and gloomy cave.
My voice echoed eerily from the hard rock walls.
My feet squelch in the icy wet water.
As I cross the slippy wet rocks I fall down and down.
My clothes feel wet and soggy as I go
Further and further into the dark and scary cave.
I wonder, am I alone? I hear something.
I go on and on until I get near light,
I am out of this dark and soggy, miserable cave.

Emel Bagdatlioglu (10)
Levendale Primary School

ALL AROUND ME

You sleep in the darkness all around,
Outside bats fly over the moon.
Inside my house the beds creak,
The clocks tick,
Pumps are on,
Chuck-a-chuck, chuck-a-chuck, all night long.
Out of bed the cold air freezes your feet.
In bed the warmth melts the cold.
Sometimes you can hear the hamster on her wheel,
Even see my brother's light on.
But all alone in my bed
I pull the cover over my head!

Lynsey Edwards (10)
Levendale Primary School

DEEP DARK CAVE

I feel nervous as I look around the dark and dreary tunnel,
Noises unfamiliar to my ears ring and echo around
the silent cave.
The world and light shut out.
Darkness all around makes me feel like I'm in a cave
with a fierce animal.
As I walk further and further I think of nice thoughts
to try and calm me down.
The blackness of the cold and clammy cave makes me
hug myself tightly.
The walls dripping wet as I walk towards the daylight.

Carly Weeks (11)
Levendale Primary School

DEEP DARK CAVE

You feel as if eyes are watching you
through the eerie everlasting tunnel.
When I shouted my voice echoed off the
damp, dull cavern walls.
It is like a roller-coaster trying to weave
through the holes and growing stalagmites.
The thin, tall cavern makes you dreary
and the blackness drowns you.
The dripping of water is the only noise
as you go deeper.
The empty, desolate landscape twists and
turns until suddenly it ends.

Stuart Stock (11)
Levendale Primary School

DEEP DARK CAVE

I saw a cave outside in the misty murky weather
and decided quickly to scuttle in, it was misty inside.
As I walked further into the mist, the dust gulped me up.
I heard an eerie scraping so I walked slowly further
into the spooky cave.
The mystery of the cold and clammy cave was sparkling with fear.
The spookiness of the sunny cave made me shiver
until my bones rattled.
At the end of the desolated cave it made me shiver until
my teeth were grinding with a magical noise.
Then all of a sudden I broke out into sparkling sunlight.
I was blinded with joy!

Lyndsay Pullan (11)
Levendale Primary School

LYING IN BED

I lie in bed,
The clock tick-tocks
The silver moon up in the sky glows
Glows in my eye
My dad's drinking beer
The glass's tinkling fills me with fear
Owls hooting
And cars tooting
At the bottom of my bed
There's a shadow, oh, it's ted!
There's a full moon
I want to be asleep very soon.

Robert Edemenson (9)
Levendale Primary School

DEEP DARK CAVE

As I walked into the cave
It sucked me in like a plughole.
I walked down the cave
With the wall as my guide.
I suddenly fell down a hole
I fell, lying in pain on the ground.
I got a burst of strength somehow
And got back on my feet.
I saw some sunlight.
I followed it, limping in pain.
As I walked out the cave,
The sunlight blinded me.

Jack Manning (11)
Levendale Primary School

THE SMELLIEST SOCKS ON EARTH

The last time I changed my socks was back in March I think,
That's March in 1985 - my goodness how they stink!
My fiendish feet give off such fumes skunks at the zoo did swoon,
In fact the dreadful odour was detected on the *Moon!*
A fellow I'd called rude names decided to attack,
Swiftly I took off my shoes and knocked him on his back,
I knew with my fantastic socks that soon I'd shoot to fame,
I told it to my teacher, he said 'Don't be so lame!'

Jack Harris (10)
Litcham CP School

A WORLD OF MIRACLES

A miracle to me is
sitting on a soft sandy
beach watching the sun
go down.
Opening colourful wrapping
paper off the presents at
Christmas,
Also I like looking at the lights
at Christmas.
Playing in the salty
wavy sea.
Bobbing up and down on the
waves,
The joy of animals making
a noise.
The joy of skiing down a
soft white mountain of
                    Snow!

Jessica Warman (11)
Mattishall Middle School

A WORLD OF MIRACLES

The sun comes up slowly, starting a new day,
Glowing on the tall trees, making the dew shine like crystal.
Animals start waking up, rabbits and squirrels come out.
People get up and start cooking breakfast,
the smell of bacon, and eggs drift out.
The sand is getting warm along with the sea,
the beaches will soon be full.
The rain starts falling while the sun's still out,
the beautiful colours of the rainbow start coming out,
brighter and brighter.
The day is getting hotter and the animals run free on
the fresh green grass.
The day is coming to a close, the sunset's colours are
spreading through the sky, then black settles on the world.
All these things are miracles trapped in

A great world!

Elizabeth Wood (11)
Mattishall Middle School

MIRACLES

The sun setting in the sky.
The water that we drink.
The animals down by the river.
The plants and trees that grow in forests.
A newborn child for a new mother.
The moon in the night sky.
God the Creator of the world.
The stars glowing in the night.
All these things are miracles to me.

Daniel Harrold (11)
Mattishall Middle School

COLOUR

Yellow, yellow,
Is the blossom on the trees.
Sad, sad,
The willow looks.
Plain, plain,
Looks the old crumbled wall.

Red, red,
Looks the robin's tummy.
Smoothly, smoothly,
It flies through the sky.
Sad, sad,
When all the birds die.

Sarah Pearson (11)
Mattishall Middle School

COLOUR POEM

White, white,
The soft fluffy clouds.
Gold, gold,
The sun shines around.
Quickly, quickly,
The plane races past.
Softly, softly,
The wind blows quietly.
Pour, pour,
The rain comes down.

Kerri French (11)
Mattishall Middle School

COLOUR POEM

Pink, pink,
Is the sky at the night,
Brown, brown,
The trunk of the tree,
Blue, blue,
Is the stream by the tree,
Yellow, yellow,
The colour of the daffodil
Red, red,
The colour of the cockerel's crown,
White, white,
The colour of the high cloud.

Sally Bangs (11)
Mattishall Middle School

YELLOW

Yellow, yellow,
The warm glow from the sun above.
Sand, sand,
As it sparkles in the midday sun.
Yellow, yellow,
The holidaymakers' chips - crisp and delicious.
Tall, tall,
The daffodil that appears in spring
Yellow, yellow,
The banana that hangs in the banana tree.
Yellow, yellow,
Is the duckling born in early spring.

Ricky Gayfer (11)
Mattishall Middle School

COLOUR POEMS

Golden, golden,
Are the stars in the darkness.
Black, black,
Is the sky under the moonlight.
Loud, loud,
Is the hooting of the owl.
Quick, quick,
Is the bat flying around.
Cold, cold,
Is the dark night air.
Sad, sad,
Is the whistling of the wind.

Gina Steggall (11)
Mattishall Middle School

RORY HARPER

R unning at the goal,
O n the ball all the time,
R oaring past players,
Y elling for the ball.

H ard on the tackles,
A way with the ball,
R egularly wearing number 9
P assing everywhere,
E asing the ball past the keeper. That proves I
R eally, really love football!

Rory Harper (10)
Middleton VC Primary School

SHSHSH! DON'T TELL MRS STEEL!

Mrs Steel thinks I'm listening,
But really I'm at home
I'm a dog, playing in the garden.

Mrs Steel thinks I'm reading,
But really I'm out on the field -
I'm Mr Steel and he's scoring a goal.

Mrs Steel thinks I'm working,
But really I'm in the war.
I'm Florence Nightingale and I'm chopping off someone's leg.

Mrs Steel thinks I'm doing art,
But really I'm Helen Whisking
Doing drill with the cadets.

Mrs Steel thinks I'm doing French,
But really I'm in space,
I'm Neil Armstrong going to the moon.

Mrs Steel thinks I'm learning my spellings,
But really I'm on my skates.
I'm Lyndsy Thorpe and I'm going to be the best skater in the world!

Lyndsy Thorpe (11)
Middleton VC Primary School

SHELL

As smooth as a pebble
Light as a leaf
Ridged like a knife
Hard as love
Rough like a road.

Jonathan George (11)
Middleton VC Primary School

COLOURS

Black is the colour of zebras grazing on the Savannah
As the sun beats down on them.
It's boiling.

White is the colour of delicate snowdrops
As fluffy, spring lambs skip about them.
It is cooling.

Green is the colour of the tropical leaves
As the animals climb through them.
It's humid.

Grey is the colour of the misty Scottish hillside,
                              dotted with heather
As the mystical mist rises.
It is damp.

Gold is the colour of the harvest leaves
As the icy wind frees them.
It is warming.

Nicola Symonds (10)
Middleton VC Primary School

SHELL

As rough as sandpaper,
Round like a football,
As cold as ice,
As brown as mud,
Curved like a stone.

Thomas Seaman (11)
Middleton VC Primary School

COLOURS

Yellow is the colour of rich sand
With my spade.
It is soft.

Blue is the colour of a bright sky
As the birds fly round and round
It is light.

Green is the colour of the grass
With flowers growing fast.
It is bright.

White is the colour of shining doves
That land on my hand.
It is glossy.

Purple is the colour when I'm happy.
It makes me glad
It is cheerful.

Amy Gurney (10)
Middleton VC Primary School

SHELL

A bumpy as a cattle grid,
As hard as iron.
As round as a circle,
Cold like frost
And rough like sand.

Andrew Turner (10)
Middleton VC Primary School

COLOURS

Blue is the colour of the cold winter's sky
As we drive to school.
It is cloudy.

Red is the colour of Megan's face when she is excited
With Barney in her hand.
It is mad!

Green is the colour of a little hopping frog
With bright orange spots on his back.
It is frog-like.

Purple is the colour of Emily's furry pen
When she tickles me with it.
It is ticklish.

Pink is the colour of my spelling book
With some crosses inside.
It is horrible.

Laura Footer (10)
Middleton VC Primary School

MARYANN

M aryann is my name
A nd I have two sisters.
R ed is my favourite colour.
Y ou are my friend and
A pples are red.
N ice to see you
N ice to be your friend!

Maryann Watkins (11)
Middleton VC Primary School

SSH! SSH! DON'T TELL MRS STEEL!

Mrs Steel thinks I'm listening,
But really I'm on Mars,
I'm an astronaut eating my tea.

Mrs Steel thinks I'm reading,
But I'm at the circus,
I'm part of the crowd eating popcorn.

Mrs Steel thinks I'm doing Design and Technology,
But really I'm in Paris,
I'm Gustave Eiffel, building the Eiffel Tower!

Kaylee Petch (10)
Middleton VC Primary School

FOOTBALL

F idget in the changing room, then
O n the field we run,
O pponents waiting on the pitch,
T hen the game's begun!
B alls flying in the goal,
A rguments with the ref,
sL iding tackles, what a foul!
L inesmen don't agree!

Sammy Reeks (11)
Middleton VC Primary School

COLOURS

Black and *white* is the colour of my horse
When he's clean.
It's good!

Red is the colour of fire
When it's hot.
It's very hot.

Green is the colour of grass
When it is growing.
It is soft.

Ben Partridge (10)
Middleton VC Primary School

COLOURS

Red is the colour of hot, burning rage
When danger lurks.
It is angry.

Black is the colour of a sad Victorian Queen
As tears settle in her eyes.
It is sad.

Grey is the colour of a stormy sky
As it thunders.
It is frightening.

Alice Rainbird (11)
Middleton VC Primary School

ALIENS

They are nice and green,
And they have a queen,
Lots of people eat pies,
Which are speckled with flies,
They all like Jim Bake,
Who looks like a cake,
There is the mad 'cusic',
Who does play the music,
They go to the moons,
Carrying the spoons,
Tom Fantastic is cool,
He even has his own pool,
His wife lady June,
Looks like a full-moon,
Sweet Mrs Skeleton,
Looks like a pelican,
I have been to space,
Now I have to face,
To go to my own home,
To see my garden gnome.

Joanna Turner (11)
Northwold Primary School

ROCKETS, ROCKETS

Rockets, rockets floating high,
Out in space diddly-die,
Coming along to the moon,
Keeping out from the tomb,
Eating, eating until we stop,
The little old moon is now to *stop!*

Paul Preston (9)
Northwold Primary School

112

SHOOTING STARS

I love to watch a shooting star,
See it go from Earth to Mars,
I see it sparkle night and day,
There it goes on its way,
I see it shimmer through the sky,
Look at it go, I wonder why?
There it goes so hot and fast,
The planet Saturn goes past,
There goes Jupiter and Uranus,
And Neptune and of course Venus,
I love to watch a shooting star,
See it go from Earth to Mars,
I see it sparkle night and day,
Now I see it on its way,
But before it goes I wave goodbye,
Before shooting stars shoot through the sky,
Bye to the shooting star,
Shooting past the planet Mars,
Please come back day or night,
I wonder if I could shoot through the sky?

Dayna Cook (10)
Northwold Primary School

THE FRIENDLY ALIENS

Aliens playing in the sky,
Look around from up high,
In the galaxy floating around,
Everyone is green and round,
Never fight or never fly,
Spacemen see them up in the sky.

Ryan Spindley (9)
Northwold Primary School

ROCKETS

Once a green, red, yellow, blue and white thing
Was flying round and round,
It's a rocket, a rocket,
It had a sharp point on its way to the moon,
It's a rocket, a rocket,
It flies very fast on its way to the moon,
It's a rocket, a rocket.

It goes up in the universe passed stars,
It's a rocket, a rocket,
Passed comets a black planet,
It's a rocket, a rocket,
It lands on the moon so dark and cold,
It's a rocket, a rocket.

On the moon so dark and cold,
It's a rocket, a rocket,
Then they just go straight home,
It's a rocket, a rocket.

Brownwyn Singleton (10)
Northwold Primary School

SHOOTING PLANETS

Space and planets Mars and Moon
The planet Saturn, Venus, Neptune
All the planets around the sun
So many here and there
You never know that they are there
Bolting around the universe such a sight to see
All it leaves is magic dust glittering like the sea.

Tim Jolly (10)
Northwold Primary School

SHOOTING STARS

Shooting stars go ever so high,
A lovely sparkle in the night sky,
Lovely colours go shooting by,
Ever so hot, oh I wish it was mine!

Shooting stars,
Moving very fast you can only see the magic dust.

Why do they fly so high?
I really wonder why?
I sit because they want to be known
I really just don't know.

On his way he sees all the planets
Including the sun and a comet.

Shooting stars,
Moving very fast,
You can only see his magic dust.

Jenna Waller (9)
Northwold Primary School

ROCKETS

Rockets are so high
flying in the sky,
like a star floating by
in the sky.

One rocket flying
so high in the sky,
so fast you can't believe your eyes.

Amy Peckham (9)
Northwold Primary School

ALIENS

Aliens have big slimy eyes,
For their breakfast they have planet pie.
When they have fuzzy fozzle juice they slurp,
And then of course an earthquake comes because they burp.
They like pepper on their cheese
But then of course they sneeze.
And along come a swarm of bees
They have red rugs
They drink from mugs
They look a big smug
When they see a fat bug.
They have six legs
Their noses look like pegs.
They also like rotten eggs
They have tremendous lips
They're for sucking lolly dips.

Francesca Eyles (10)
Northwold Primary School

PLANETS IN THE SKY

Planets planets in the sky,
Going fast around the earth,
Never crashing into anything.

Rockets in the sky,
Moving about in thin air,
Because there is not much gravity,
Then it comes down like an aircraft.

Steven Milner (10)
Northwold Primary School

SHOOTING STARS

The shiny stars keep on glowing,
People can see they are showing.
Shiny gold, yellow and silver,
Every day they're coming nearer.

The shooting stars are fast and big,
Shooting stars play games of tig.
Shooting stars are made of gas,
But I don't mean made from grass!

Shooting stars are really fast,
I hope they will ever last.
Spacemen want to visit them soon,
Then back onto the moon.

Lovely stars come out at night,
In the morning they say goodnight.

Abigail Chilvers (9)
Northwold Primary School

BLAST-OFF

Blast-off!
The booster's engaged,
Yellows, oranges, reds blasted from the boosters.
The rocket lifted-off the podium with stars and sparks flying,
Armstrong and Aldrin cry a yipee!
The controller says
'Houston has ignition!'
Armstrong and Aldrin see a pearly spot in the distance.

Samuel Ward (11)
Northwold Primary School

SHOOTING STARS

The shiny stars glide through the sky,
While the people down there,
Are looking up high.

The golden stars,
Fly through the pitch-black sky,
The sparkling stars whisk past the gloomy moon.

The glowing stars shoot past all the planets,
Then they just reached Pluto with the very cold climate.

The bright yellow stars flicker,
In the dark black night,
Oh no!
The stars go,
Here comes daylight.

Michael Waring (8)
Northwold Primary School

SPACESHIPS

Spaceships zoom through the glittering stars,
Flying down to Earth from Mars.
The shimmering space craft is twirling right down through
The black sky,
It twirls and burns and wanders by.
It starts to turn and heads my way now,
It sees a landing place where it can lay.
It floats right down and starts to rest,
Which now starts to go to the big windy west.
The engine goes down and the astronauts frown and look
And say 'That was a superb day.'

Cara Taylor (10)
Northwold Primary School

AN ALIEN IS GREEN AND SLIMY

An alien is green and slimy
And plods along very slowly.

An alien jumps up and down
When you call him names,
He will frown.

This alien has a space dog
And this alien's name is Bob!

When he grows up
He will go off in a spaceship
To see the snow.

An alien is green and slimy
And plods along very slowly.

Dale Ward (10)
Northwold Primary School

THE LION

His pointed claws are as sharp as knives.
Ready to pounce on anything that's moving in the jungle.
Small beady eyes, they're little round marbles that move.
Shiny white teeth as clean as a new shirt.
He furiously bites his prey.
Round and round he goes looking for his dinner.
His stringy tail is a floating piece of rope.
He's leapt and killed a little creature.
Now he's going to rest and will be back tomorrow.

Rohan Jadhav (11)
Norwich Road School

JELLYFISH

Its sting is sharp and cruel.
An Australian sea wasp jellyfish
Can kill in just a few minutes.
Mean, powerful
Nothing can stop it stinging
Any day, any time.
The jellyfish will leave a scar
A mark of remembrance for eternity
A tentacle trap
A hanging fringe of poison
The longest death whips in the underwater world.
His head is a hemisphere floating and flapping
A ball of jelly
A foul flavour to taste
An open gliding umbrella.
Deep, deep down in the bottom of the sea
Sometimes peacefully sleepy
But one foot comes and collides with its sleep
He wakes up furiously
The poison shoots out
But bloodthirsty and deep.

Shakira Simone Garrett (11)
Norwich Road School

RAT

His orange beady eyes are burning like candles in the dark,
As he rummages through daylight.
The rat's teeth are like a blunt knife, nibbling away scrap on the floor.
His rough, bald fur is like a dirty rag just lying on the floor.
Pointed claws are like a kitchen knife just from the packet.

Joe Peaks (10)
Norwich Road School

THE SAD LION

The lion's overgrown claws were as sharp as a bird's beak.
His big black nose, as cold as an ice-cube.
Big strong feet as big as a bike tyre.
Bushy fur like summer trees in full bloom.
He pines for his mum as they took him from the wild jungle.
He felt unhappy and sad.
Will he and his mum escape?

Kristan Dicker (10)
Norwich Road School

THE WHITE TIGER

The pointed claws are like razor blades shining in the sun
As he looks down and licks his paw.
His round beady eyes watching the world.
And twitching ears are like radars listening for something.
The big white tiger pounces like lightning
And catches his meal in the African heat.

Tess Marples (11)
Norwich Road School

THE HYENA

The hyena's spotted coat is like a rug with ink blots on it.
His ear-piercing laugh is like an emergency siren.
He prowls the land looking for dinner sneakingly.
Those glaring eyes show how scary he is.
They glow like fireflies in the misty night.

Simon Smith (10)
Norwich Road School

THE FOX

There is a red,
There is a blue,
Lots of people like foxes,
Them and me too!

The blue, a cloud
On a rainy night.
The red runs hot,
As a flash of light.

The blue seems evil,
The red seems good,
They are both on the prowl
Opposite sides of the wood.

The sun goes down,
They're both alone.
The two retreat,
And howl and moan.

Lauren Shanahan (10)
Norwich Road School

THE QUIETEST THINGS IN THE WORLD

The quietest thing in the world is a slug
Or a snail slithering on the ground.
Or a ladybird, very nice and round.
Butterflies with colourful wings are quiet.
Or a little mouse or a fish.
And a rat.
But all these things are quiet.

Kati Brooks (8)
Norwich Road School

MY GERBILS

My gerbils are brown and grey
My gerbils are light
They like to play
Especially at night.

They run round their cage
Squeaking and eating
They run on their wheel
Then they get tired.

They sleep all day
So then they are quiet
When they wake
They cause a riot.

Ben Burris (8)
Norwich Road School

HAPPINESS IS . . .

Happiness is watching TV.
Happiness is being Maxine's friend.
Happiness is going to the fair.
Happiness is playing in the snow.
Happiness is going to Centre Parcs.
Happiness is going to school.
Happiness is swimming twice a week.
Happiness is Mum, Dad and my sister.
Happiness is eating chocolate cake.

Kimberley Watkins (8)
Norwich Road School

THE RABBIT

The rabbit's twitching nose is like a pneumatic drill,
      going up and down
      sniffing, sniffing.
His marvellous tongue is licking the water bottle furiously
      tasting, tasting.
The tall ears of the rabbit are hearing carefully,
      twitching at every sound
      listening, listening.
Gleaming eyes are looking desperately at the house
      waiting for his owner
      watching, watching.
Waiting for his five minutes of freedom out of his small
      cage into the large garden.

Michelle Deborah Smith (11)
Norwich Road School

THE HAMSTER

The old hamster will sleep all day,
He sleeps where nobody can see him.
At night he will come out and play,
He will scamper over to his food dish,
Getting bits of food in his small hands.
He will put it away in his cheeks for when he gets hungry.
The playful hamster goes on his wheel
Round and round and round all night long.
As he wobbles round his cage his little nose twitches,
Whiskers are long and very bushy,
He sniffs round everywhere to see what he can find.

Clare Nicholls (11)
Norwich Road School

THE AWFUL WEDDING

The groom's in white, the bride's in grey,
A dreadful start to a terrible day.
The sun has gone in and it's starting to pour.
The best man's drunk, and on the floor.
Uncle Bert is feeling ill
Aunty Glad has gone for a pill,
The bridesmaid's got a runny nose,
A split in her dress, a hole in her hose.
The vicar hasn't even come,
Funny that neither's Mum!
It's not quite the day we'd hoped it would be,
Let's grab uncle Bert and go home for some tea!

Raisa Taher (11)
Norwich Road School

A NEVER ENDING FLOOD

When it waves backwards and forwards
It comes closer and closer every day
I wished it would go away!
I won't see my house again
Go away you dreadful water
We want our home back.
I wished for 20 years it would go away
But it wouldn't push.
I ask it again another 20 years
But it still didn't push.

Michael Burris (10)
Norwich Road School

POWERFUL SPIDER

The spider's thin legs are like a tooth pick.
His triangular eyes are as small as a full stop
on the end of a sentence.
The spider's small hairy legs are like my grandad's head
when he is relaxing in bed
The spider's powerful sting is like getting an electric shock
from 10,000 volts.

Daniel Greenwood (11)
Norwich Road School

MY LITTLE RABBIT

The big feet on her, so long she can trip over them
As she is hopping around in her run.
She has fur as soft as a feather pillow,
Her floppy ears are nearly as long as her.
The small rabbit's little bobtail is like a bit
Of cotton wool stuck on her.

Heidi Teixeira (11)
Norwich Road School

THE ANGRY TIGER

In the Indian desert the tiger's claws
Were razor-sharp like a kitchen knife.
As fast as a motor bike driving in speed traffic.
The big hairy tiger has black stripes on its body like a zebra.
His scary teeth are as dirty as mud when he scares the whole town
Away in anger and fear.

Ejaz Anwar (10)
Norwich Road School

THE HUNGRY CROCODILE

His sharp teeth are like knives hanging,
Waiting to cut something up.
The crocodile's blue eyes looking out for prey.
Getting hungry, but he knows it will come.
Its long, green body, sitting waiting for dinner.
There it is he thinks, he moves in 'Gulp'
He moves his small legs down the bloody river.
Looking out for more, one creature is not enough.

Jordan Harden (11)
Norwich Road School

THE GIRAFFE

The long colourful neck as bright as fifty glowing lamp posts.
Its big round eyes black and gold.
As kind as a monkey being fed.
The huge skinny legs as tall as the highest mountain on a winter's day.
Its round stumped nose as heavy as a bookcase.
As freely as a tiger in a jungle.

Terry Cooper (11)
Norwich Road School

THE LION

The lion's big claws are sharp to kill the other animals in the forest.
His pointed teeth are sharp enough to eat any animal that is dead.
Its soft fur is as warm as a blanket on a radiator.
Eyesight is good enough to see in the night
Lion's get beaten by other lions and then they are lion's meat.

Mark Le-Vine (10)
Norwich Road School

THE DOLPHIN SWIMMING IN THE SEA

Its rubbery flippers are as streamlined as an aeroplane structure.
The dolphin's words are loud cries of communication.
They travel for miles, until they reach the path of the finder.
Their tiny teeth can be as sharp as a knife when chewing prey.
The wide open ocean is like an African Savannah with animals
Of beauty swimming around.
The dolphins will come up out of the water for the magic air
They will need to continue their journey through the open seas.

Sarah-Jane Currie (10)
Norwich Road School

BULLDOG

A bulldog is a lovely mammal.
Fur as soft as a feathered pillow,
If he sees someone he doesn't know
He will bark, growl and loudly bellow.
His flabby skin is like a winter coat
Makes him sweatier than a rabbit or a billy goat.

Mark Snowdon (11)
Norwich Road School

THE OWL

His yellow eyes are like the sun beaming down on you,
Its knife-like claws to get his food,
In less than seconds the food died,
Its sad cry is like a baby's cry,
The tired owl, closes its eyes and falls asleep.

Leiat Becker (11)
Norwich Road School

THE SNOWMAN

It was a cold snowy day
And I was sitting outside
I was bored
I wish I was inside
I am as white as a feather
I am a snowman
I have two coal eyes as black as space
And two buttons as round as a ball
And a carrot for my nose as pointed as a sharp knife
And one snowy day the sun same out
And melted all the snowmen.

Dean Constantinou (11)
Norwich Road School

HAPPINESS IS . . .

Happiness is eating ice-cream on a sunny day.
Happiness is going on a hot holiday.
Happiness is eating chocolate and sweets in the car.
Happiness is listening to my Spice Girl's CD
Happiness is watching TV.
Happiness is when we are not in school.
Happiness is with your best friends.
Happiness is when it is Christmas and you get presents.
Happiness is when you go swimming in the sun.
Happiness is when it is a hot day.

Sasha Bradley (8)
Norwich Road School

CREATION OF WINTER

Is snow just a blunder?
Did God send it down
A clown that didn't know what to do?
He said 'The world, the world,
It seems so dull
I'll make it shine,
With something called snow,
Not too bland,
But something quite majestic.
It will gnaw the ground,
Swirl, swiftly, softly, silently, then suddenly
Children will play with snow every day.
I will nip their fingers, they will cry for mercy,
They will go indoors, when their finger go red raw.
I'll come down heavily
Drown all the dead leaves.
Under me will all be covered
Unknown to man or woman.'

James Lyall (11)
Norwich Road School

STEPPING OUTDOORS IN WINTER

I step outdoors in winter.
Frost and snow attacks my toes like wolves biting.
The winter wind rushes through the tree leaves.
The snow falls softly as it lands on my face.
The pond is a glacier that is melting.
The rigid, frozen icicles drip onto my head.
Winter has wrapped the garden in a white sheet.

Craig Flude (11)
Norwich Road School

MY KITE

As high as clouds,
As low as grass,
You dive and swoop,
Slow and fast.

I lost mine,
When I took it flying,
Shame you know I ended up crying.

Simone Archer (9)
Norwich Road School

THE PONY

What the pony eats is grass, hay and wheat.
The grass is like a blade of a knife,
The hay is plastic tubes,
The wheat is like the sun shining in the field.
It runs like lightning
Its teeth are like cubes
Its eyes are beads glowing under the moon.

Jamie Roe (11)
Norwich Road School

THE SPLASHING WATERFALL

I am a waterfall
Splashing and twisting down rocks
I dance and glance on my way
When I get to the end of the waterfall
I shoot quickly into the stream
I am a water beam.

Victoria Louise Hawks (10)
Norwich Road School

WATERFALLS

Waterfalls are high crashing waves
Waterfalls form
ponds
streams
lakes and rivers.
They are so powerful
They are so magical
But they are crystal clear
Splashing droplets
moving fast
in the air
but then they just disappear.

Montanna Harden (9)
Norwich Road School

WINTER WIND

Swish, swish,
What am I?
I am the wind
I steal people's houses.
Smash their roofs,
Tear their trees down.
But I can also blow the snow.
I breathe a gentle breeze,
And lift the birds,
And sigh in the trees.

Andrew Hopkinson (10)
Norwich Road School

THE CAT

The cat is a powerful figure,
Always prowling around,
Always on the go.
Its silken whiskers,
The best in the world
Its miaow a cry
Everlasting.

Its underneath as soft as the softest fur,
Glamorous to touch.
A *hunter!*
The face of an angel,
But a killer's heart.

Simon Cooper (10)
Norwich Road School

WINTER WIND

The bold brave wind
Blows wildly
Whistles through tree-tops
Whips us waves
From nowhere,
From everywhere,
The bold, brave wind dies out.
Suddenly the surprising sun
Shoots out from the distant galaxies
The sun spreads a smile on everyone's face
Brightening everything in its path.

Katy Peters (10)
Norwich Road School

DO DRAGONS EXIST?

'Do you know what ice is?'
Asked the human child.

''Tis the dragon's claw, sharper than any glass.'
'Then what is the rain?'
''Tis the dragon's sorrowful tear that fills a sea of pain.'

'What is the snow?
'It is an icy winter dragon's scales that cover the
Aged earth.'

'The leaves that fall to his mercy
They bind to make his frozen skin.'

'The wind?'
''Tis the dragon's icy breath, bleaker than any arctic country
'But where have all the dragons gone?'
'Man has killed them all, all except for one . . .
. . . Winter.'

Charlotte Banks (11)
Norwich Road School

MY SILENT WORLD

N   o sound,
O   nly silence,
S   ilent world,
O   ut of touch with people,
U   nderstanding my world is hard.
N   oiseless,
D   eafness.

Louise Cotton (9)
Norwich Road School

AUTUMN

Autumn is
red, green and yellow leaves
and acorns falling from the trees.

Autumn is
conkers growing on the trees
and falling with a thump.

Autumn is
cold and windy.
I have to wear my warm blue coat.

Autumn is
leaves blowing around,
they make circles in the sky.

Amy Dalton (8)
Norwich Road School

ENCHANTED LAND

Down dark in a magical land
    Lies a prince in need of a hand.
    In need of someone, something.
The bells give an ear-piercing *bong!*
Between the increasing mist
Hoot, hoot cries the old owl
    All at once galloping, galloping
    Then lock the enchanted land disappears
But a figure is emerging in a silhouette black
    Then galloping off to meet her
Prince is last at broken enchanted land.

Amy Russell (9)
Norwich Road School

THE POLLUTION OF THE SEA

The sky is painted on my face
The dolphins swimming,
As my grace.

The killer whale swims through
Me
Leaps up!
And splinters my face so gracefully.

An oil ship came,
And leaked its oil
To ruin my mane
And also to spoil.

It spread by far, and stuck like tar,
It ruined me, it killed me
And all the animals in me

No sky on my face,
    No dolphin grace,
        No killer whale to splinter
            My face.

Gavin Edwards (10)
Norwich Road School

WINTER

Whooshing winds blow all around
In the winter snow
No leaves on the trees
Tiny snowflakes falling and the
Earth is covered with a blanket
Round the whole wide world.

Dane Clears (8)
Norwich Road School

THE WORLD OF SILENCE

T he world is quiet to me
H ere I am all lonely
E verybody misunderstands me and

W hat I'm going through.
O r they just ignore me because of my disability.
R ight now I can't hear anything but myself.
L uckily my teacher helps.
D ifferent I am not, to her

O f course it is hard for everyone to know what I am saying.
F irst I really want to be liked and treated normally.

S econdly I would like to have friends.
I f only I could hear what people say.
L ike, I could hear what my teacher says.
E ven if people whisper I could hear a little bit.
N ow I don't think that I'll ever hear.
C ures - will anyone ever think of one?
E ven if it takes a long time, I hope they find one for people
   who are deaf.

Hollie Stocks (9)
Norwich Road School

SNOW BEAR

Silently, snowflakes settle
Tiny cloud pieces
Falling, floating, drifting
To join other flakes on the window sill.
Covering the hard ground,
Like a snow bear,
Hugging the earth.

Robert Lee Davis (10)
Norwich Road School

WISHES

I wish I had a very good
    friend who
      I could trust.

I wish I had a pet pig
    so we could play
      all day.

I wish I could help
    the poor
      and old.

I wish I could sing
    like the pop group
      Aqua

I wish nobody had to
    die.

Melissa Norman (8)
Norwich Road School

TEN TORTOISES

Ten tortoises talking to the television.
Twenty tigers tickling toes.
Thirty thrushes thinking thoughtful things.
Forty flamingos fighting four fish.
Fifty foxes' fierce fever.
Sixty sea lions swimming stupidly.
Seventy squirrels scoffing spinach.
Eighty elephants eating evergreens.
Ninety newts knitting nasty noses.
One hundred hedgehogs hurrying home.

Ben McCarthy (8)
Norwich Road School

THAT REALLY MAKES ME *MAD*

Every time I go out on the streets
And see people cry.
The thing that makes me really mad
Is that they don't eat pies.

I try to make them eat pies
But they don't take any notice.
But the thing that makes me really mad
Is that they said 'I'd rather be at the Post Office.'

I said to them 'Don't go to the Post Office
They won't give you any money.'
But the thing that makes me really mad
Is that they said 'We're going to get a bunny.'

'Don't worry I'm going to stop you getting that bunny'
'Oh no you won't because we're in a hurry'
'Oh that really makes me *mad*.'

Victoria Blackmore (10)
Norwich Road School

THE SEA OF SNAKES

The sea is like a swirling snake
Slithering down the way
Wriggling over dead fish
Brushing against sharks
Slashing my tail from side to side
Clashing my jaws up and down
Swishing over sand
Crashing onto rocks.

Katherine Elizabeth Pizzey (10)
Norwich Road School

SHE'S HERE

Deep sense of purple in the house,
A feel of evil came upon me,
The smell of death from the door.
'Come child, come now
For I won't hurt you.'
'What's happening?'
Sound of drums,
Beating slowly as the witch comes before me.
The witch I saw, was it a dream?
Is it real?
I woke but where?
Cold, dirty room
Smell of rats and damp.
'Dear child have you woken.'
I didn't dare to speak.
Witch with long fingers
Black, dirty fingernails
Stirring up trouble in her cauldron
'Child come, sit next to me
Have a drink'
'What is it, poison?'
'Drink up?
She watched as I drank.
Face wrinkly, spotty with a smile
I felt like life had stopped.
Then all of a sudden I let out a cry.
'No don't hurt me'
'Don't do what?'
How, what, why?
The witch stood, took her broom,
Flew
Minutes later she's back,
With another child.

I know this is my last time alive.
'Come child, come to me now
For I won't hurt you.'

Catherine Russell (12)
Norwich Road School

SPIDER IN THE GARDEN

The lights are out
The sun is down
His colour is a misty-brown
Spider in the garden.

His web is like a spaghetti maze
He ambushes his prey
He has his ways
Spider in the garden.

His pin-shaped teeth like deadly daggers
His venom is a can of acid
The bloodthirsty savage, he prowls
Spider in the garden.

His tiny eyes are inky spots
Seeking for his prey
They vainly struggle to get away
Spider in the garden.

He believes he is unbeatable
As he scampers through his territory
But bigger eyes are watching
The spider in the garden.

Stevie Higgins (10)
Norwich Road School

MY SILENT WORLD

N o friends
O nly silence

S omebody please sign to me
O nly my family like me
U nderstand me, I'm deaf
N o one likes my
D eafness

I am very, very sad

A lone
M iserable

D eaf
E everybody thinks I'm different
A world of silence
F rightened.

Natasha Wren (9)
Norwich Road School

ASKING QUESTIONS

How can people build liners?
Why are people different?
Why do birds go tweet,
Who invented electricity?
How many schools are there in the world?
Why are there lots of countries?
Who invented God?
Is there a pot of gold at the bottom of a rainbow?
How does the world go round?
Why is there salt in the sea?

Bethany Reid (8)
Norwich Road School

MY SILENT WORLD

M yteries all around.
Y ou can't hear anything.

S ilence everywhere.
I feel frustrated.
L isten, I wish I could.
E very day something new happens.
N o one understands what I'm going through,
T raffic, you can't hear it.

W onderful world all around me.
O nly I know how it feels to be deaf.
R ain, can see it but not hear it.
L onely life when you can't hear.
D on't ever hear the birds sing.

Katie Wordley (9)
Norwich Road School

THE MYSTERY BOX

The mystery is inside the box
In the corner of my sister's room
Once I tried when she was sleeping
But then got told-off
For peeping.
I had a smack and was sent to bed
But it still plays in my head
She takes it everywhere, school,
The park, *everywhere!*
Tomorrow I'll smack her
And smack the box with her hammer
What is in it?

Ryan Lott (10)
Norwich Road School

NOWHERE TO RUN

There be a witch,
Who lives with trolls,
So I was told,
By Aloyo the elf,
Found a spell of hers,
This is what it said.

Leg of Eggno
Heart of dwarf
Brain of dragon
Gut of Griffin
Stir them up in my cauldron
Death spell for the king.

Nowhere to run,
Nowhere to hide,
I silently wait in fear,
For her to come,
I'll know when she's near
She carries the evil smell of death,
On her rags,
Wherever she may be,
Nowhere to run,
Nowhere to hide . . .

David Vickers (12)
Norwich Road School

IS SHE A WITCH?

Accent chills my bones.
High voice making my ears pop.
Is she a witch?

Red before her purple eyes.
Burning wart before her ugly face.
Looks like a hideous hag.
Is she a witch?

Long fingers.
Long nails.
Craving itch upon her spotted head.
Smell of death on her rotting rags.
Is she a witch?

Square feet rotting like a dustbin.
Black teeth below her purple eyes of death.
Rat's blood in her cauldron.
Stirring it up to make a hideous potion.
Is she a witch?

Evilest woman in the world.
She's a witch.

Carl Campbell (12)
Norwich Road School

THE SEA

Waves reaching 12 foot high
Nearly, nearly
Touch the sky
Swirling, whirling
Crashing, smashing
Boats and beaches
Take a bashing
A change in the
Weather makes things better

Dolphins jumping
In and out
Cruise boats
Slowly moving out
The sea has now
Calmed right down
Dolphins swimming
Round and round
The sea's a lovely place to be
So please don't be scared of me.

Bethany O'Donnell (10)
Norwich Road School

DEAF

Now I cannot hear.
Outside I can hear no one.
Sound was nice, but I can't hear it.
Our world was nice.
Unhappy I am.
No one likes me here.
Die, I want to die because I am deaf.

Christina Gabell (9)
Norwich Road School

DON'T LOOK!

Walking in woods
Don't look!
Trees singed by burning eyes,
Scary laughs,
Having fun,
Little steps,
Seeing horror,
Cauldrons full,
Nail-less fingers,
Pulling a face,
Mask!
Feeling spotted,
Run away,
Ugly hags,
Prepare to kill,
Don't look!

Kim Reeves (12)
Norwich Road School

BEING DEAF

N ot hearing your teacher is so horrible,
O r a car coming towards you.

S ound I cannot hear,
O h I do hate being deaf,
U nhappy, oh I do feel unhappy,
N ot hearing your mum or alarm clock in the morning,
D eafness, I do hate it.

Matthew Wright (9)
Norwich Road School

WHY IS THE SKY?

Why is the sky blue?
Why? Why? Why?
Is it because God made it blue?
Tell me why.

Why is the sky so high?
Why? Why? Why?
Is it because we may hit it some day?
Tell me why.

Why is the sky there?
Why? Why? Why?
Is it so we don't float into space?
Tell me why.

Carly Sargeant (8)
Norwich Road School

BEING DEAF

N o I can't hear any words
O r even my mum saying a word

S o I have to read her lips!
O r I have to read a paper
U able to hear a thing
N o cats, buses, vans or birds singing in the morning
D eafness is one thing you would not like to have.

Paul Kybird (9)
Norwich Road School

WISHES

I wish I drove a Lamborghini
Shooting down the road.
I wish the poor had money too.
I wish I met my uncle
Robert before he died.
I wish I was rich and had
A mansion.
I wish I could be a
Builder at eight years old.

I wish I could fly in
The sky and could
See the clouds.

Lewis Archer (8)
Norwich Road School

DEAF

N ot hear the doorbell
O h deaf, deaf

S ounds I cannot hear
O h trouble, trouble
U nlucky I am deaf
N ot hearing the telephone
D eaf, it's me.

Christopher Cooper (8)
Norwich Road School

A LITTLE BIRD

I have a little finch
She is no more than an inch.
When I came back from church
She was sitting on her perch.
She makes a lovely sound
She only cost a pound.
My neighbour Phil
Has a bigger bird named Bill.
He always talks
But sometimes walks
And this is the sound he makes
Clip, clop, clip, clop.

Natalie Lewis (9)
Norwich Road School

NO SOUND

N o sound.
O nly silence.

S ilent work.
O nly quietness, no one.
U nderstands me.
N ever hear anything
D eathly silence.

Stacie Milne (9)
Norwich Road School

SLEDGING

I silently slid down the slippery hill
Covered in a fluffy, white duvet of snow
I sit on the back of the sledge
As it gallops gallantly
I glide through the galaxy
Icicles prickle my nose
I break
I halt
Frost-bitten feet tingle
I go home
The night devours the
Snow.

Nathan Ross White (10)
Norwich Road School

DEAF

D eaf, deaf, deaf, oh why me?
E ven though I'm a nice child.
A day is impossible to enjoy.
F antasies are dark, always sad.
N ever a lovely day.
E ven a trip to the zoo is upsetting.
S ound is a thing of the past.
S ad, always sad, no happiness.

Michael Flynn (9)
Norwich Road School

MY DEAFNESS

My life as being deaf is sad
You can hear me but I can't hear you

Deafness is fun to have,
Every day is fun,
A friend will be kind to me whenever I am scared,
Forever I will be like this,
Never ever will I cry,
Everyone is kind,
Silent is my world,
Silent is my day.

Lucy Hills (8)
Norwich Road School

DEAF, DEAF, DEAF

Deaf, deaf, deaf, oh why me?
Everywhere I go I feel lost.
Angry, I feel angry!
Fantastic world it must be.
Nothing is nice.
Everyone takes the mickey.
Silent, that is what my world is like.
Sad, that's what I'm like.

Zoey Flint (8)
Norwich Road School

ASKING QUESTIONS

Who invented the rainbow?
How many stars are in the sky?
Who invented the sun?
Why is there winter?
Why are there schools?
Why do elephants squirt water?
How does the moon look like it's moving when it's not?
How do stickers get sticky?
How was rock made?
Why do people get different jobs?

Georgina Riches (8)
Norwich Road School

DEAFNESS

D eaf, deaf, deaf. It has to me
E ven though I don't deserve it please.
A nybody go away the deafness
F or it isn't very nice at all.
N o it isn't nice. I can bid on it Jeaf.
E vans is the name isn't it? Pardon?
S imon, I am deaf, okay go away.
S im you see.

Karl Brooker (9)
Norwich Road School

WISHES

I wish I was a fairy
to do good deeds around the world.
I wish I could drive a car
a nice silver Rolls Royce.
I wish I had a younger sibling
to take care of while Mum was at work.
I wish I had a pet unicorn
to ride up to the field.
I wish that we had our own house
so we can get a dog.

Lauren Gordon (8)
Norwich Road School

A DEAF MAN WALKING DOWN THE STREET

A deaf man walking down the street,
Very happy has a pet.
I wonder why he's so happy to be deaf?
Well I know why he's so happy.
It isn't because he's deaf no, no.
It's because he can play games with other people,
Like Scrabble, Cluedo and Ludo.
So maybe when you're deaf, I suppose that it isn't so bad being deaf.

David Browne (9)
Norwich Road School

IF I WAS A BIRD

If I was a bird
my wings I would spread
I'd swoop over you
and plop on your head!

You'd think I am naughty
you'd think I am bad
It's only nature
and you've been had!

Christopher Edwards (8)
Norwich Road School

WINTERTIME

When the ground is white
And it's very cold
Children play outside
They play snowball games
And have snowball fights

When the trees are bare
And frosts are growing
What do we do all day
Do we sit indoors
And wait for spring
No, we go out in the snow

Hills are glistening in
The snow
Sledges going down in
Rows
All enjoying snow rides
Before it goes.

Andrew Dobosl (10)
Ormesby Middle School

FADE AWAY

I like to swim,
I like to dance,
I like to eat my tea.

I don't like curry,
I don't like beef,
And black is not for me.

I like maths,
I like RE,
And I simply adore Leonardo DiCaprio.

Games are so boring,
Especially in the wind,
It's better inside,
With a good book beside me.

But best of all,
When I'm at home,
I love to play with my friends,
We listen to Backstreet Boys,
And eat pancakes,
And all of my dislikes just
Fade away.

Maria Murphy (11)
Ormesby Middle School

EXCUSES

I didn't do my homework
because I wasn't hearty
'cause when I came home from school
I went to a surprise birthday party.

I didn't do my homework
because this time a sinner
but my excuse this time is
I went out for dinner.

I didn't do my homework again
you may call me a clown
I went to the pictures with my mum
and her stupid car broke down.

This time it's my fault I made a hash
instead of doing my homework
I went to splash.

This is my last verse
I would like to say sorry to the nation
I know it's my fault
but I spent too much time on the PlayStation.

Lee Jeffries (12)
Ormesby Middle School

LIKES AND DISLIKES

McDonald's can be really fun,
To eat a burger in a bun,
And if I didn't have to pay,
I'd be in there every day.

You may think that I'm quite a nutter,
Because I hate the taste of butter,
So in the kitchen I am seen to eat dry bread,
No margarine.

I must admit I love my food,
And can eat greens if in the mood,
But I find my greatest treat is loads and loads,
And loads of meat.

My sister can be quite a pain,
My brothers something else again,
Between them both they drive me wild,
Why was I not an only child.

Sometimes happy, sometimes sad,
But I'm glad I've got my mum and dad.

Amanda Copestake (12)
Ormesby Middle School

LEAVING TREES

Autumn's here the leaves are falling,
Leaves are falling down,
Colours changing all the time,
Making a patchwork on the ground.

Like traffic lights the colours alter,
From grassy green, amber and red,
Soon faded yellow and then to copper,
Till rusty brown and nearly dead.

Now the leaves are off the trees,
And now they are crunching, tired and dry,
Then the wind comes and they start to dance,
Tossing and turning I wonder why.

The tree is now bare without its coat,
A shadowy silhouette scraping the sky,
It's like a skeleton with twig like fingers,
And arms for branches reaching ever so high.

Thomas Hall (12)
Ormesby Middle School

CLUTTER ON MY BOOKCASE

Screwed up paper.
My dad's old stapler.
Old wooden train.
Small golden chain.
Pass the pigs game.
New wooden frame.
Picture of me.
Stains from my cup of tea.
Old fashioned cars.
Book on the planet Mars.
Real gold frames.
Video games.
China frogs.
Plastic hogs.
Biscuit crumbs.
Old china drums.
Old piggy banks.
Plastic army tanks.
What a mess.

Ben Stone (12)
Ormesby Middle School

SUMMER SEASIDE

Sun gleaming down below
Sparkling, glittering
Waves crashing, splashing
Against glistening rocks
Rays reflecting, bouncing
Off the shining sea
Different shades of colour
Red, yellow, purples
Oranges and gold
Birds singing
Children building castles
Collecting shells
Paddling in the silver sea.

Apryl Markham (9)
Ormesby Middle School

PARENTS

Ask yourself each one of you,
Who is there when you need someone the most?
Who comforts you when nothing seems to go right?
Who's always willing to give advice?
Who helps you when you're stuck on homework?
Who steers you right away from wrong?
Who nurses you when you're ill?
Who works so you can enjoy life?
Who can you rely on to be there for you?
Parents that's who!

Thomas Pearce (11)
Ormesby Middle School

DRY

As dry as the dessert sand.
Sometimes hard as land.
As dry as the leaves on the autumn trees.
Which blow down in the breeze.
As dry as the light wind.
When the sun shines on the tin.
As dry as a biscuit.
Would you dare risk it?
As dry as a bone.
When talking on the phone.
As dry as an engine without any oil.
As dry as a kettle, no water to boil.

Avril Lacey (11)
Ormesby Middle School

STALLION

I am a stallion, I run free,
So why can't the other horses be like me?
Wild and free,
They call me Snowy the stallion because I am white,
I never, ever bite.
Give me a friend to graze in the meadows with
or to drink from the stream with.
As if it was all just a dream
Please set the horses free,
For they will come back to you you'll see.

Kylie Hall (10)
Ormesby Middle School

DON'T JUMP ON THE CRACKS

'Don't jump on the cracks,'
said Johnny Jacks.
'I won't,'
said Sally Ront.
'I won't either,'
said Tommy Teither.
'Neither will I,'
said Polly Tye.
'Are you sure?'
said Danny Pure.
'Yes,'
said Lynne Ress.
'Course we are,'
said Robert Far.

'Don't jump on the cracks,'
yelled Johnny Jacks.
'We aren't,'
yelled back Betty Larnt.
'Look you are jumping on the cracks,'
said Noddy Pracks.
'Oh yeah he is as well,'
said Becky Daswell.
'So don't tell us not to jump on the cracks,'
said Timothy Bracks.
'He's blushing,'
said Dinah Crushing.
'Cor he is as well,'
said Becky Daswell.
'Oops I just jumped on the cracks,'
said Timothy Bracks!

Ashleigh Rouse (9)
Roydon County Primary School

GOING TO THE FAIR

We are going to the fair today
On a hot summer's day to go on the new roller-coaster, Zola Bay
The dodgems, the Ferris wheel and lots more
We are going to the fair today
To see the lion with the scary mane
We are going to the fair today
To go on the ghost train when it starts to rain
Bang goes the thunder and the rain
We are going to the fair today
To try and win some goldfish
Nothing only a cuddly fish
Time to go home now
Goodnight.

Paul Mackmin (9)
Roydon County Primary School

HORSES

H umungous horses galloping around the field.
O range horses carrying around knights with a shield.
R iding the horses up and down.
S eeing the horses going round and round.
E legant horses walking very posh.
S ent to the stable to have a wash.

Melissa Eaton (9)
Roydon County Primary School

THE GOBLIES

The Goblies are mean and green
Disgusting and sickly and rude
If you get in their way
They might take you away
So never, ever intrude
They creep and crawl
From wall to wall searching for a victim
I once saw a man park in a white van
And they all came out and nicked him
They have got a red glow
They like to eat flies
The Goblies, the Goblies, the Goblies.

Matthew Oxley (8)
Roydon County Primary School

MY CAT

My cat Fluffy
Is a very friendly cat
She sleeps near the fire
She goes out at night
To hunt for mice
She always brings them home
She is very furry
She is as black as coal
I love her very much.

Sherree Larter (9)
Roydon County Primary School

THE DAWN BIRD

The dawn has come
The birds have gone
But all except for one
He sits on a tree
Calling for company
But no other bird comes
So he just sits there
All the other birds come
They cheep and they chirp
And sing and flap
And how good it was
To have all your friends back!

Lucy Harbour (8)
Roydon County Primary School

HENRY VIII AND HIS WIVES

Henry VIII had six wives,
but none of them had long lives.
The first one was Catherine of Aragon,
but when they divorced she was gone.
The next was Anne Baleyn,
but when she was beheaded she was no longer queen.
Jane Seymour was the third,
she gave birth to a son and died.
Anne of Cleves was next,
but they divorced because Henry was vexed.
After that was Catherine Howard,
perhaps when he beheaded her she was a coward.
Henry's last wife was Catherine Parr,
he died first, so she went far!

Gus Eldridge (10)
St Nicholas School, North Walsham

SAFARI PARK

My seat belt is fastened,
I am eager to go,
The engine has started,
But the animals lie low.

I look for the lions
With their cubs so small,
I can see the giraffes,
Because they are so tall.

We drive to the lake,
For a trip on the boats,
In the water are sea lions
With their wet and silky coats.

We get off the boat and into the truck,
I want to see rhino
With their magnificent horns,
But they see us first and away they go.

It's the end of the outing,
And as we drive back,
We see baboons in the distance,
As we drive down the track.

Rupert Smith (10)
St Nicholas School, North Walsham

BABIES

Goo, goo gaa, gaa
Goo, goo, gaa, gaa
that's how a baby goes
Goo, goo, gaa, gaa
Goo, goo, gaa, gaa
with a runny nose

Babies are so very happy
until they have a dirty nappy
change it as quickly as can be
boy it is so smelly

Now it's time for a bath
washing your hair is such a laugh
splashing around is so much fun
wrinkly fingers mean you're done

A bottle of milk warmed just right
settles you down for the night
snuggled down in your bed, cuddled up to big ted
hopefully a good night's sleep ahead.

Oliver Brighton (10)
St Nicholas School, North Walsham

SANDWICHES

Cheese and onion with salad cream,
Egg and cress would be my dream,
Beef and pickle on pitta or rye,
It doesn't matter if the bread's a bit dry.

Most people like sandwiches for lunch,
Or if they got up late they make it their brunch.

There are many fillings you can put between slices or crust,
But my favourite is chicken, that is a must.

Children like chocolate, spread nice and thick,
Older people are fussy and like to pick,
Some sandwiches can be toasted like cheese and ham,
Or maybe you like sweet things like honey and jam.

Robert Bird (9)
St Nicholas School, North Walsham

THE TREACLE PUDDING

When my mum makes a cake
It has the lovely smell of sweets
So I quickly jump off the sofa
And ask her what it is
She says it's a treacle pudding
And I say that's my favourite
So after tea we have my favourite pudding
That treacle pudding
And at the end I have treacle all around my mouth
So after that I wash my face
And go to bed
And dream about
That treacle pudding.

Leanne Ditch (9)
St Nicholas School, North Walsham

THE SEAGULL FLYING

Soaring through the blue sky,
At a great speed,
Going across the deep ocean,
On my flying great seagull,
Her feathers fluttering back into my face,
And her great big wings flapping,
We are landing in the ocean now,
Gently gliding along,
Then night falls,
The moon is out,
And the stars twinkling away,
We close our eyes,
Slowly drift off to sleep,
Dreaming and contented on the ocean deep.

Jennie Hall (10)
St Nicholas School, North Walsham

MUM!

Mum hoovers the house and the mouse
Mum feeds the chickens without them licken
Mum shops and drops
Mum reads the books and then she cooks
Mum x-rays on Sundays
Mum gardens all day to get it out the way
Mum makes the pond (while I watch James Bond!)

Mum does the dishes while I play with the fishes
Mum has no time to think but occasionally she has the odd drink
Mum takes me out and about when I have on my face a pout
Mum takes me swimming and then to Burger King
Mum is the best - that does not rhyme with the rest.

Ryan Price (11)
St Nicholas School, North Walsham

ON SAFARI

Up in a tree a monkey I see,
a little fur ball looking down at me.

As tall as a tree a long neck does rise,
a neck of a giraffe with its big, beady eyes.

From behind a lake a long nose rises,
a squirt of water which does cause surprises.

Then I hear loud, loud stamping,
the elephant and rhino their big feet tramping.

The zebra galloping faster and faster,
the hyena behind cries lots of laughter.

All the animals the big and the small,
No doubt about it, I like them all.

Caroline Chapman (10)
St Nicholas School, North Walsham

DOGS

Terriers are loyal and cheerful
Highland Terriers are barking mad
Collies have a lion's mane
The tallest dog which was recorded was a Great Dane
Newfoundlands are usually black and look like small bears
But they normally eat everything (but my dog won't eat pear)
Labradors make excellent guide dogs for the blind
And the Retriever, gentle and kind
Watch out for the fierce Rottweiler who might be behind!
Chow Chows have a black tongue and are very cute
when they are young
Dalmatians are very spotty but sometimes a little dotty.

Rachel Stone (9)
St Nicholas School, North Walsham

MY MUM

My mum's a very special person,
She likes to laugh and have fun,
But she doesn't get much time to do that,
Because she's always on the run.

I have 2 sisters who are very annoying,
We sometimes fight and complain,
But mum always manages to sort it out,
However much we moan.

We have 12 pets, I feed 4,
But my sister Zoë's at boarding school,
Amy's too busy going out to Norwich with the boys!
My dad he has to work all day,
So really, you see, poor mum has to feed the other 8,
Poor mum, she really is a saint!

Holly Dunham (11)
St Nicholas School, North Walsham

THE DREAM

Here comes a big banging lorry,
and here I am in the middle of the road.
Here comes the lorry smashing up the road,
a big, great black lorry coming towards me now.
Now another lorry is joining it,
and another and another, there is now a group of lorries
coming towards me.
They're a metre away now and here I am in the middle of the road.
Bump - beep, beep, beep, beep.
Oh my brother's alarm clock.

Alastair Cockburn (8)
St Nicholas School, North Walsham

MY DREAM HORSE

My dream horse would have to be
A palomino called Rusty

We'd run around in the fields all day
We'd jump, canter and we'd play

Our favourite game would be to race
We'd race the fastest horse called Lace

Sometimes we'd win, but never lose
'Cause Lace would always break the rules

We'd enter in a running race
And if we told her so would Lace

The track would often be quite dusty
But he'd still win, would my horse Rusty.

Zoe Stennett-Cox (9)
St Nicholas School, North Walsham

TOFFEE THE BARMEY CAT

Toffee is so barmey
He runs around the house
Running through the bathroom
And chasing bumble bees.

Toffee causes havoc
Everywhere he goes!
He's either in the flowerpot
Or biting Pepsi's nose.

Mum gets very angry
Dad he gets so cross
Sarah thinks he's funny
But Kirsty knows he's boss!

Toffee is a hooligan
But that is not the point;
The whole family loves him
Till he steals the Sunday joint!

Benjamin Brown (11)
St Nicholas School, North Walsham

LITTLE AND LARGE

Every day at school
Someone calls me tiny or small
But I just wish
That I could grow big
(So no one could call me small any more)

I wish every night that I could grow tall
On the star which is biggest (but I still stay small)
My friend Rupert is big you might have known
But if I was him I might grow
(So then no one could call me small any more)

If you are small just like me you shouldn't care
You probably think that life is not fair
But no matter where you are or what you do
There is always someone worse off than you.

Simmo Catchpole (10)
St Nicholas School, North Walsham

CANDY

I have a pony,
she is pure, pure white,
I take her out for a ride
after school every night.

She is a Welsh Mountain pony,
with a long, long tail,
I feed her tea in a little red pail.

She sleeps silent at night,
in her open bay,
in the morning I give her hay.

In her stable there is straw,
but in the morning
she asks for more.

Chantelle Prior (11)
St Nicholas School, North Walsham

NORWICH CATHEDRAL - THROUGH THE WINDOW

I look through the window at Norwich Cathedral.
A baby crying, children playing.
Guides teaching, children learning.
People praying, having services.

Lots of people walking around with car keys.
The organ playing, playing sweet songs.
Children waiting, waiting for their lunches.
I go away from the window and I'll be back tomorrow.

Helen Fogg (9)
West Raynham VC Primary School

THROUGH THE WINDOW - NORWICH CATHEDRAL

Through the window I did spy
Into the past I went by and by.
Saw some people through the stained glass,
Spied some movement - at last!
People shuffling to and fro,
Others going somewhere I don't know.
A woman crying 'My husband has died.'
A monk came to comfort, he died in pride.

Now back to the present,
Where people more pleasant live.
A school on a trip,
Taking a sip - of the Cathedral's past.
I pull my face from the window now,
And wonder, oh how, oh how?
The medieval builders were so good at things,
That we can do, but nearly need wings.

Amazing I say
Amazing once more
Now I know history
Is
Not
A
Bore.

Ashley Balderstone (11)
West Raynham VC Primary School

NORWICH CATHEDRAL - THROUGH THE WINDOW

I look through the window
and what do I see?
Some people singing softly.
There's some people over there praying quietly
And now the bells are ringing loudly.
There's a school group over there
Looking around the Cathedral.
This wall is very dull.

I look through the window
and what do I see?
The walls painted beautifully.
The organ is playing and people are singing
But no chairs to sit on
Not one.

Donna Wright (10)
West Raynham VC Primary School

NORWICH CATHEDRAL - THROUGH THE WINDOW

The monks come into sing and pray
The bishop is leading the service today
The walls are painted red and gold
The monks are very bald

The alien tourists visit earth
The cathedral stands in its turf
The earth is 3,000,000 years old
Still the Cathedral stands with pride.

Ashley Craine (11)
West Raynham VC Primary School

NORWICH CATHEDRAL - THROUGH THE WINDOW

I look through the window
And what did I see?
I saw a monk looking at me.
I saw the building nice and colourful.
I haven't ever seen a building so high.
I look through the window
And saw a service going on.
They say the prayers and sing the songs
I heard the bell ring loudly.
They get up at 2.00
And have their dinner at 12.00.
I look through the window and what did I see?
A monk dancing at me.

Diane Flinders (10)
West Raynham VC Primary School

NORWICH CATHEDRAL - THROUGH THE WINDOW

Through the window what do we see?
A bishop taking a service with thee.
The man and the organ watch how he plays.
The guide said this is the way.

See the men pull the stone,
While they make a dreadful groan.
Up comes the boat from Normandy,
That sailed along the deep blue sea.

Matthew King (9)
West Raynham VC Primary School

NORWICH CATHEDRAL - THROUGH THE WINDOW

In the window everywhere
People walking here and there
Children rushing everywhere
Babies crying! Lots of people sitting down
Everyone singing and another day has gone

Hear the bells ringing
People coming in
People singing hymns and songs
The sun is shining in the sky
Birds are singing outside.

Matthew Jolliffe (11)
West Raynham VC Primary School

FOX

Glowing amber eyes appear
The tip of tail white
She had caught a hare on the run
Then her sleek outline disappears
To soothe the cry of her young
I followed totally amazed
To see a perfect den
A smell so strong filled my nostrils
I gasped to see the fox on watch
And the vixen licking her cubs
Then suddenly dawn appeared
And the foxes disappeared
I trudged home with the sight in my eyes
A fantastic night for fox watch.

Emily Nichols (10)
West Winch County Primary School

ONGIG

'Twas Tudor times in 1509,
King Henry on the throne.
Busy town including rats and mice,
Other animals too and smells.

Beware of the Ongig, my friend,
Those snapid jaws,
Those stoodum claws,
If you don't beware, higaboom you're gone.

He took his stoodum sword
And rested in the candubee tree.
Nobody messes with Grall
Or higaboom, you're in heaven.

Boom! Boom! 'What is that?' said Grall.
He fell out of the tree.
He saw the Ongig.
Snapid! Snapid!

Ongig licking his lips.
Higaboom! Higaboom!
Grall said goodbye to the Ongig
And Grall went running back with a leg.

'Twas Tudor times in 1509,
King Henry VIII on the throne.
Busy town including rats and mice,
Other animals too and smells.

Thomas Eaton (7)
West Winch County Primary School

THE MOON SHINES DOWN

The moon shines on the rooftops,
Every night and day.
The moon has got a beautiful shine,
It shines on the street lamps every night.

I can see the security man lock up the shops.
I see children going to sleep.
I can see the bright stars all around me.

The moon has got a face.
The moon is big and fat at night.
The moon shines over the whole street.

I wish I could land on the moon.
I wish I was a spaceman.
I wish I could go to Mars.
I wish I could land on Mars.

Jake Veal (9)
West Winch County Primary School

THE FOX

Stealing and jumping
and thumping and chasing
its tail around and around
before it's bound
crashing and bashing, tumbling and grumbling
before it's bound, fishing and wishing and hissing
and christening before it's bound, crying and buying
and frying and flying before it's bound.

Layla Andrews (10)
West Winch County Primary School

BELLE

I once knew a dog called Belle,
She had no home of her own,
She spent her days playing with children,
And her nights in a barn alone.

She relied on others to feed her,
But never begged for more,
You just knew Belle was hungry,
When you heard the scraping at the door.

I know I will never see Belle again,
She's part of my distant past,
But I have my photos and memories,
And they will always last.

Annika Hambilton (10)
West Winch County Primary School

THE THING IN THE CHURCH TOWER

And moving through the chiming bells,
the thing in the church tower emerges.
Spirits cry out to the silent town,
and terror comes to haunt.

The frightful creature from the church
is the nightmare in your mind,
along to the town goes the thing,
to catch the caring, good and kind.

Alison Belton (10)
West Winch County Primary School

THE MOON

The gleaming moon shimmers bright,
when the sun has set and the night
passes by.
The glowing moon must be lonely,
nobody to look at apart from still life
and houses, but only a few
moving cars.
But what will happen to the silver moon
in the future?

Disappeared, destroyed, bombed.
What do you think?

Rachael Eaton (10)
West Winch County Primary School

MY LIZARD

(In memory of Valcor)

My pet, my lizard,
Isn't much of a wizard,
Of biting or much else,
But in this special creature,
There is a special feature,
He has such a gentle heart.

My lizard, my pet,
You can't see him on the Internet,
He is hard to find,
Because he's one of a kind.

Rebecca Yare (10)
West Winch County Primary School

ANIMALS

There are animals that are fluffy.
Scratchy, lazy, sleepy and stupid.
There are some animals that like grass.
Some animals like cats and dogs.
Cats are sometimes daft and trouble.
But dogs are mean or tame.
Ginger, black, brown and white.
Dogs can be called
Marmalade, Singe, Chester and Chulney.
Cats can be called
Willow, Blossom, Lazy, Fatty
Or instead, I think a proper name.
You can choose a name for your pets.
Unless it has a name
Already.

Cindy-Louise Stewart-Whyte (9)
Wicklewood GM Primary School

MY HORSE AISHA

A horse chomps all day, even in May.
Bucks and rears, chomping near.
Laying under a chestnut tree, a chestnut mare does appear.
On the mountain late at night, a horse sleeping soundly
in pale moonlight.

Joanna Berger (9)
Wicklewood GM Primary School

MY PETS

My rabbit is black.
He is as black as a chimney.
He pinches carrots and
lettuces out of the garden.
He goes next door and
tidies the floor.
My cat is grey, she's out
hunting all day.
She'll bring back mice in
a trice.
My fish are long, my fish are short.
They swim backwards and forwards
quick and slow.

David Bush (9)
Wicklewood GM Primary School

HEDGEHOGS

Hedgehogs hide until the night.
They are nocturnal people say.
But when they eat they never have
beans on toast in the day.
In fact they do not eat them anyway.
But they do eat beans.
I think it's time to say goodnight
and the hedgehogs say good day.

Kathryn Beckett (8)
Wicklewood GM Primary School

MY DOG

My dog is a cocker spaniel.
He's black and white.
He runs fast as a cheetah.
He has floppy ears long as paper.
He hates water.
He likes catching birds to
Have for a present in his bowl.
He is cuddly, he never gets angry.
And he's a good friend.

Sebastian Cardew (9)
Wicklewood GM Primary School